GOD

IS FOR

EVERYONE

Paramhansa Yogananda

GOD
IS FOR
EVERYONE

INSPIRED BY
PARAMHANSA YOGANANDA

As Taught to and Understood by
His Disciple, J. Donald Walters
(Swami Kriyananda)

CRYSTAL CLARITY PUBLISHERS
NEVADA CITY, CALIFORNIA

Cover design by C. A. Starner Schuppe

Original cover photography of Ponte Vecchio,
Florence, Italy, by J. Donald Walters

ISBN: 1-56589-180-5
Printed in the United States of America

Crystal Clarity Publishers
14618 Tyler-Foote Road
Nevada City, CA 95959-8599

Phone: 800-424-1055 or 530-478-7600
Fax: 530-478-7610
E-mail: clarity@crystalclarity.com
Website: www.crystalclarity.com

Library of Congress Cataloging-in-Publication Data

Yogananda, Paramhansa, 1893-1952.
   God is for everyone / inspired by Paramhansa Yogananda ;
as taught to and understood by his disciple, J. Donald
Walters (Swami Kriyananda).
      p. cm.
Rev. ed. of: The science of religion. 1920.
Includes index.
   ISBN 1-56589-180-5
   1. Religion. I. Walters, J. Donald. II. Yogananda,
Paramhansa, 1893-1952. Science of religion. III. Title.
   BL48.Y5 2003
   294.5'4--dc22
                                    2003016049

CONTENTS

PREFACE

This book was first intended to be a slightly polished version of Paramhansa Yogananda's first literary offering, *The Science of Religion*, which he published in 1920 before coming to America from his native land, India. Instead, it has become a new book. The message, though expanded upon, is the same, though I don't suppose a sentence of the original remains. I have written it as though it had been penned by Yogananda himself. This method has often been employed by disciples of a great master. In Paramhansa Yogananda's *Autobiography of a Yogi* we are told that his guru's guru, Lahiri Mahasaya, would sometimes tell a disciple, "Please expound the holy [scripture] stanzas as the meaning occurs to you. . . . I will guide your thoughts, that the right interpretation be uttered."* In this way, Yogananda continued, many of Lahiri Mahasaya's perceptions were recorded

*First Edition reprint, Crystal Clarity Publishers, p. 40.

and published.

Though all my books represent a conscious attempt to be an instrument for his teaching, it must be said that this one has been more so. It was a sincere effort to rewrite his book for him — as a ghostwriter if you like, though he isn't physically here to check my efforts. I present it as his book because all the ideas are, deliberately on my part, his own. This present version will, I hope, be easier to comprehend and more enjoyable to read. For although the first edition contained wonderful teachings, it stated them so weightily that many a daunted reader has not remained with it to the end.

The Science of Religion has never sold well, a particularly unfortunate fact in light of Yogananda's clear intention, through this book, of reaching a broad audience. That tens of thousands in America later attended his lectures, and that many of them became his students, makes it all the more important that the message he expressed in this book be disseminated, now, as widely as possible.

In 1955 I was discussing editorial matters by telephone with Laurie Pratt, Paramhansa Yogananda's chief editor. Today, Miss Pratt is better known by her monastic name, Tara Mata. I knew her then as Laurie. She lived a quasi-hermit's life, and rarely communicated except by phone.

During our discussion she remarked, "I'm

thinking of dropping the publication of *The Science of Religion.*"

"Why on earth?" I cried in dismay. "Its message is *central* to Master's* teachings!"

"Master never actually wrote it," she replied. "It doesn't even have his vibrations."

This book had always been a favorite of mine—not for its style, perhaps, but certainly for its contents. "Who did write it, then?" I demanded.

"Swami Dhirananda," she answered. This monk had been summoned to America by our Guru during the 1920s to help him with the spread of his work. Dhirananda had departed the scene, however, long before my own entrance onto it as a disciple in 1948. His name was only dimly familiar to me.

"The very writing style," Laurie continued, "is Dhirananda's, not Master's. It is heavy and pedantic, and betrays the pride he felt in possessing a master's degree. Even his choice of words projected none of Master's charm and simplicity. *The Science of Religion* reads more like a scholarly dissertation than as a work of deep inspiration!"

"But in its *ideas*, at least," I protested, "it has to be Master's! For that reason alone, surely, it would be a pity simply to drop it!"

*"Master" was the term of love and respect we disciples used when addressing our Guru, and when speaking about him among ourselves.

Perhaps my dismay influenced her. At any rate, the book continued in print. Her comments also, however, remained firmly etched in my memory.

I learned a little more about Dhirananda's role in authoring *The Science of Religion* during four years that I spent in India in the early 1960s. There I had occasion to speak with Swami Satyananda, another of the Master's early companions. Satyananda told me, "After Yoganandaji's return from his visit to Japan, which he describes in *Autobiography of a Yogi*, he was inspired with insight on how to reach a worldwide public with the message God had given him. Accordingly, he wrote an outline of those ideas in Bengali. He didn't yet feel capable of writing them in English, however, so he asked Swami Dhirananda, a member of our little group, to write them in English as a booklet."

Dhirananda, in other words, was the ghostwriter; the truths expressed were all Yogananda's. A human being is not the clothes he wears, but the living person inside them. The inspiration for *The Science of Religion*, similarly, was Yogananda's; Dhirananda only tailored the suit.

English usage has changed over the past eighty years. Dhirananda's somewhat cumbersome style is now outmoded. Nor was it ever elegant, and the suit he tailored was always a poor fit. The coat, moreover, with its excessive repetitions of concepts, had become frayed at the elbows, rather like a professor's old jacket at the twilight of his career.

In fairness, I must add that Daya Mata, the president of Self-Realization Fellowship, has disputed my claim that Paramhansa Yogananda did not actively author this book. Dhirananda, she insists, was its editor, not a ghostwriter basing his work on Master's notes. I can only say in reply that I have expressed my own very clear memory of both Laurie Pratt's and Swami Satyananda's comments. I have no wish to argue this point, so will leave it to the reader to decide which version he prefers.

In May of 1950, Paramhansa Yogananda gave me instructions for my own future service to his mission. "Your work," he said, "will be lecturing, writing, and editing."

I hesitated over that second item. "Sir," I said, "haven't you already written everything that needs to be said about your teachings?"

"Don't say that!" he exclaimed, surprised at my obtuseness. "*Much* more is needed!"

Since that time I have devoted my life to carrying out those instructions. My books, which at present number more than eighty, have been written primarily to interest people in his teachings. I have tried also to show that his insights lead irresistibly to ever-broader conclusions. My efforts have been rewarded in that they have, so far, reached millions of readers—not only in English, but (as of this writing) in twenty-seven other languages. I have also edited a book of conversations that I and others had with our Guru, which were published under the title, *The Essence of Self-Realization*. Finally, I have edited what, to me, is a veritable scripture: Yogananda's *Rubaiyat of Omar Khayyam Explained*, on which task he got me started a few months before our conversation quoted above. My earnest prayer has always been to reach a wide audience with his teachings, and to demonstrate in addition their immense practical value in people's daily lives.

I was recently again reading *The Science of Religion*, when the thought came to me, "Laurie was right! The ideas expressed here are wonderful, but they don't touch the heart." I then thought, "Would it be presumptuous of me to attempt to rewrite this work?" I prayed inwardly for guidance.

The present edition is the result of that prayer. This is still my Guru's work, though it has been extensively rewritten. Even though thoughts have been expressed in new words, and stories added to illustrate the points made, I've tried conscientiously to express only *his* ideas. Most of the stories were ones he himself often related—to everyone's delight, for even when imparting deep wisdom he could be marvelously entertaining! I've done my best to present his concepts as he himself might have done, with the fluency he later achieved in English. And I've tried to convey some of the inspiration that we, who heard him, invariably felt when he spoke.

I encountered more difficulties with this project, however, than I'd expected. I've always been comfortable with editing his words, so rich with wisdom. Indeed, they have become my whole way of life. I found it a challenge, however, to separate his ideas from interpolations added by Dhirananda.

Eventually I found it necessary to go through the text with a view not only to improving its style, but to clarifying its concepts. I've replaced whatever lack of clarity I found in Dhirananda's version with Yogananda's actual teachings as I understand them from years of study and experience, and from my numerous conversations with him.

It might help the reader if I explained further why Laurie would have even considered dropping the publication of this book. The sad truth is, Dhirananda, some years after arriving in America, betrayed his guru. Ambition, and consequent envy, are unfortunately not unheard of among the disciples of great masters. (Consider Judas Iscariot's historic betrayal of Jesus Christ.) When a disciple gives precedence to his ego over his discipleship, he sometimes attacks his guru as if saying, "All that I've gained has been by my efforts. I alone, therefore, deserve all the credit." The enlightened teacher meanwhile, himself free from all ego-prompted desires, views ingratitude even in its extremest form of treachery as a spiritual disease, which he must eventually cure in his erring disciples.

Dhirananda went so far as to try to encompass Yogananda's financial ruin. That our Guru continued to keep this book in print is, to my mind, an example of the extraordinary magnanimity I always beheld in him.

It has been my utter joy to work on this book—renamed now, *God Is for Everyone.* The concepts it expresses deserve the best possible treatment. I prayed constantly that my Guru guide my thoughts during the months I labored on this project. Now that it is finished, I pray deeply that my humble efforts have pleased him.

With heartfelt sincerity,
J. Donald Walters (Swami Kriyananda)
Ananda Village, Nevada City, California

GOD

IS FOR

EVERYONE

CHAPTER ONE

Religion: a Universal Need

This book has been written to demonstrate that religion is a pragmatic necessity for everyone: that God is deeply relevant to every life, and is by no means the side issue so many people try to make Him.

If we accept that He exists, it surely goes without saying that He cannot be some minor or merely local deity. In the vast universe revealed to us by modern astronomy, God can only be thought of as infinite. To describe infinity adequately, however, would be impossible. Language derives from shared experience; it is not adequate for describing cosmic verities. The clearest mind could not conceptualize a state of consciousness that is both infinitely large and infinitesimally small—and that confounds reason itself, moreover, by being *neither* large *nor* small! The Bible describes the futility of any such attempt. "My thoughts," it says in Isaiah 55:8, "are not your thoughts, neither are your ways my ways." Mere thought could not span the abyss between finitude and infinity.

Nevertheless, there is something in human nature that feels imprisoned by finitude. Deep inside us we long to embrace infinity. We will never be satisfied until we have unraveled the mystery of existence. For man, despite Darwin's disparaging verdict, is more than animal. Everyone pondering life's strange twists and turns must surely ask himself sometimes whether there isn't some higher reality: wise, kindly (so he hopes!), and forever aware of his individual existence.

Most people think of God only vaguely, if at all. They may imagine Him as in some obscure way omnipresent, omniscient, and omnipotent. They may think of Him more personally, though still vaguely, as "all-merciful," or "all-wise." They may endow Him mentally with a form of some sort. In any case, they usually separate Him from daily reality as they know it.

This book offers an alternative to all such abstractions. What purpose is served, indeed, by holding God at a distance? Theological definitions may persuade us to bow before Him in reverence, but they cannot inspire us to love Him. Religiously inclined people may consider it excessively familiar to address Him as their very own, yet, if He created us, how can He be *anything else?* Why do we today, influenced by an ancient tradition, address Him still in the familiar form as "Thou"? Perhaps, somewhere in the past, God's closeness was more generally accepted. In any case—at least in today's English—"Thou" is no longer used. Even in conversation with our own nearest and dearest, this form of address seems to us unsuitable, because strangely formal. Indeed, one wonders whether even in olden times the familiar way of addressing God was not rather an affirmation suggested by saintly preceptors, instead of a reflection of the way most people actually thought of Him. For people also thought of Him, then, as the almighty Lord—not a concept, surely, to inspire intimacy!

It is easier, in a sense, to visualize God in the starry heavens than in our own homes. The stars, so remote from humdrum earthly existence, suggest to our minds perfect stillness, harmony, and wisdom. By contrast, our homes are often scenes of strife and rivalry. Yet if God's omnipresence includes the stars, He must also be right around us—even (as Jesus Christ put it) *inside* us. Moreover, were we able to view the stars up close we would see them to be blazing furnaces, where violent explosions erupt constantly—hardly scenes of stillness and harmony!

In any case, we cannot be forever contemplating the heavens. To the extent that we hold

God aloof from our daily realities, we alienate Him from us. We need a concept of God that will bring Him into our kitchens, our bedrooms, our living rooms—yes, even when those living rooms are crowded with guests. If God is everywhere, He must be quite as near to us as He is far away. We need to make Him our *immediate* reality. We need to seek His guidance and inspiration in our most intimate thoughts and feelings; relate to Him when the world is most demanding of our attention; seek His influence even in light undertakings; listen for His laughter behind our silliest jokes, and ask Him to infuse with *His* love our tenderest sentiments! If we don't see our need for Him simply in order to *exist*, we reduce Him to a mental abstraction: useful in mathematics, perhaps, but lacking in closer significance for us.

Ultimately, God alone can satisfy our most personal needs. In our dealings with other people, He is our conscience. In our labor, He is our satisfaction. When we read a good book or listen to uplifting music, He is our inspiration. In everything we do, from the performance of serious duty to the most trivial pursuits, He is there, watching, joining in if we invite Him to, and giving us our strength. To ignore Him means to go stumbling blindly through life, unaware of innumerable pitfalls on the path before us.

People distance *themselves* from God when they think of Him abstractly. Perhaps they imagine their belief will "save" them, but without love, what could salvation itself be? Theological definitions give no comfort to the heart. They are like antique chairs placed about to be seen, but not sat upon! Again, they are like precious chinaware, stored away safely in cupboards, but seldom used. People remember God during their times of suffering—but otherwise? In grief they may take Him out of that cupboard, dust Him off, and examine Him more carefully. Usually, however, they consider themselves well enough off without Him, as they go trudging wearily from one crisis to another, their brows furrowed in anxiety.

We need a concept of God that will *motivate* us to *love* Him. He is, even if we know it not, our very own. Do we, however, perceive ourselves as *His* own? We ought to, for so we are.

What I plan to do in this book is introduce a concept of God that will inspire you to *want* to know Him. Once you have this knowledge, it will be your fault alone if you think Him far away. *How you relate to Him is crucial to your happiness.* To define Him with hairsplitting exactness may puff one up in pride, but it will offer no nourishment for the soul. Even to long for God, though one receive no response from

21

Him, is incomparably more fulfilling to the heart than any pursed-lips acknowledgement that, "Possibly — indeed, I may assert with a modicum of confidence that *something* must actually exist 'up there,' in regions subtler than any with which humanity is at present familiar."

The theologian presents his "proofs" and syllogisms — to what practical purpose? Even he, however, must smile indulgently when he sees his little daughter playing with dolls. Will he accuse her of lavishing affection uselessly on inanimate objects? Let us hope not! Wise and learned he may be, but as a human father he must recognize that her affection, though offered only in play, helps to prepare her for motherhood later on.

In her childish games she may also learn something else: the importance of loving without any thought of return. The ability to love selflessly is a sign of maturity. Whether the love is given *wisely* is another matter — a lesson reserved, perhaps, for higher schooling in life.

In religion, similarly, the most important thing is to love selflessly.

A materialist in India once remarked to me scornfully: "Someday you and others who dedicate yourselves to the search for God will be very disillusioned, when you wake up to the discovery that He doesn't exist."

"You may be right," I replied smiling, "but at least we'll have the satisfaction of knowing that we've done some good!"

Ultimately, the main beneficiary of every good deed, and the main victim of every harmful one, is one's own self. Obviously, the question of God's existence *is* important. More important to us first, however, is that we develop in understanding. Whether He exists is meaningful primarily to the degree that we are *conscious* of His presence. Our first need is to develop our awareness. That little girl's love for her dolls is indeed, in a sense, requited: Love itself is her reward. As the poet Tennyson put it, "It is better to have loved and lost than never to have loved at all." Where true love—not passion, and not desire—is concerned, neither subject nor object really matters. What counts is love itself.

In religion, similarly, when people claim to have accepted Krishna, Rama, Buddha, Jesus Christ, or someone else as their "personal Savior," what matters is the depth and purity of their love. *Whom* they accept is less vital to their salvation than the question: Am I, myself, acceptable to God? God doesn't need reassurance that we find Him acceptable! What He wants from us is our love, reciprocating the love He has ever given us, His human children. If our *way* of worshiping Him is incorrect, but the love of our hearts is selfless and pure, He will have no difficulty in correcting our error.

Whenever I hear the expression, "Praise the Lord!" the image comes to my mind of the Lord as a rich, pampered lady craving flattery as her social due! God doesn't need our *praise!* He is, in Himself, completely impersonal; that is to say, He wants nothing: He simply *is.* In compassion, however, He is deeply personal, especially in what He wants for us: our fulfillment in perfect bliss. Otherwise, He is like a radio station broadcasting on the "wavelength" of superconsciousness. We need to tune our mental "radios" to that frequency, lest we receive some other program out of the many that are broadcast on the "airwaves" of consciousness: selfish ambition, desire, arrogance, sectarian intolerance — the innumerable distortions produced by delusion. Unless our motives are pure, we may find ourselves attuned to one of these aberrations, and delude ourselves that we are receiving "inspiration."

How can we distinguish between false and true inspiration? As you'll see in these pages, it depends always on whether the program we listen to influences us to live more narrowly centered in our egos, or more expansively in a self that embraces ever-broader realities. Egotism is self-imprisoning. Humility and heartfelt kindness, on the other hand, are liberating.

Every human being must discover what is, for him personally, most deeply meaningful. The more self-honestly he can address this question, the sooner he will find the way out of his dark cave of delusion into the clear light of understanding.

If what is most meaningful for you is the possession of money, visualize yourself as possessing it in superabundance. Ponder, then, the consequences of that excess. Would it make you truly free, or happy? Would you even be its possessor? Or would you be enslaved by it? An excess of wealth is suffocating. Your long-lasting needs lie far from hoarded wealth. A greater satisfaction than gloating over coffers of inanimate jewelry and gold is the innocent enjoyment of life itself. Such has been the discovery of everyone who has ever had an opportunity to make the comparison. Be pragmatic in your seeking! Be completely honest, as I said, with yourself. In the following pages, we'll explore further ramifications of these concepts.

This book is being written also for another purpose: to emphasize the commonality of all true religions, which aim to uplift the human spirit, though many of them, unfortunately, polarize it with bigotry and intolerance. Too long have religious leaders sought the bedrock of their faith in dogmatism. It is time they realized that religion can and should promote universal harmony. The pages of history are stained with the blood of countless atrocities — sad consequences of clinging blindly to untested beliefs. This narrow attitude is certain to change, as people's realities become more global, transformed by rapid travel and ever-speedier communication. Humanity is sure to ask itself increasingly, "How fundamental, really, are our differences?"

God is one. Truth is one. In material science the proofs of hypotheses are accepted as conclusive. Simple experimentation is the key to universal agreement, no less so as former notions of material substantiality are replaced by the knowledge that matter is insubstantial. The human body, so real to our senses, is now known to consist mostly of space. If people everywhere could be persuaded to submit their religious beliefs to the test of actual experience, they would find that dogmas constitute only a crust that covers an essentially formless reality. Many religious differences might then be resolved, for in human life the counterpart of scientific experimentation is the test of experience.

Even the teachings of various religions, each of which claims to be inspired by divine revelation, would merge in a unanimity of understanding. For the revelations themselves only *declare* truth: They do not, in themselves, define truth. Truth, like gas, which conforms to the shape of its container, is abstract. Those who know truth express it according to people's capacity for understanding.

Ram Proshad, a great poet-saint of India in the eighteenth century, showed his awareness of this fact. Though a devotee of God in the personal form of the Divine Mother, and blessed frequently by visions of Her, he sang in one of his well-known songs, "Oh, I know that a thousand scriptures declare Thee to be beyond all form (*nirakara*). Nevertheless, appear to me as the Mother I adore!"

People's different opinions about God need not be mutually contradictory. A study of the lives of those who have deeply lived their religions—the genuine saints, who appear from time to time in every religion*—reveals numerous points that they had in common. Among those similarities is an appreciation for divine aspiration whatever the form it takes, and a gentle disapproval of narrow-mindedness. The

*Paramhansa Yogananda, in common with most Indians, considered someone a saint who lived in the grace of God. Sainthood did not, in his eyes, require formal canonization by the pope of Rome. While I myself was living in India during the 1960s, a Catholic priest from Belgium challenged me, "Just what do *you* mean by the word, 'saint'?" I replied, "My reference is to the ancient Sanskrit, *sant,* from which our own word is derived. One is a saint who, regardless of his formal religious affiliation, is holy in the sight of God." —*JDW* difference between being conscious of God's presence and merely serving Him busily suggests that a more enlightened understanding may someday inspire in humanity everywhere a spirit of religious friendship and cooperation.

Human nature is infinitely complex—unlike that of lower life forms, whose responses are simple and more uniform. Even low life forms are not uniformly predictable in every reaction, the origin of which is an imperceptible center of individual consciousness.

Differences of belief among the world's religions are inevitable. Indeed, they are desirable. For God's expressions are ever unique. No two snowflakes are ever exactly alike: no two eyes, no two voices, no two thumbprints. The amazing variety in the universe should inspire people to a deeper appreciation for one another, without judging anyone. Only egotists want mirror images of themselves placed all around them—like Rameses II and his ubiquitous, self-laudatory statues. What a world it would be, were it not for life's infinite variety! What a world, indeed, if everyone wanted, let us say, to be a streetcar conductor! Religious differences, once it is recognized that divine aspiration exists everywhere, ought to increase people's appreciation for truth in all its manifestations. For those manifestations are like the facets of a diamond: displaying brilliance and beauty from whatever angle the stone is viewed. If God and truth are one, a sincere desire for understanding cannot but lead to an awareness of that oneness, and to an appreciation also for its endlessly varied manifestations. Language itself expresses similar concepts variously. The English word, *love,* means essentially the same thing as the French word, *amour,* and as the Sanskrit, *prem.* Despite their various shades of linguistic meaning,* all these differences express a universal feeling of the heart. What, except pride, can induce people to denounce one another in the name of one, universal God?

Every religion teaches, in fact, the same basic principles. God may be approached variously, but there is not one religion that tells its votaries to hate, steal, or view with indifference the sufferings of others; to suppress those ruthlessly who hold opinions different from one's own. Emperors lusting for conquest may demonstrate such behavior, but the wise? Never! No one ever pairs wisdom with contractive attitudes such as bigotry, cruelty, and intolerance. There is a well-known saying, "Handsome is as handsome does." It may be said with equal truth,

---

Prem, for example, means spiritual love, without any limitation of ego-consciousness, and certainly without emotional passion.

"Wisdom is as wisdom manifests."

Hinduism, Buddhism, Judaism, Christianity, Islam—every true religion, in fact—is no merely cultural phenomenon. It is dedicated to doing the divine will, which is ever to uplift human consciousness. Could any religion take out a divine patent on what simply IS? Humanity has one common Father/Mother, whom it calls variously God, *Dio, Dieu, Gott, Bog,* Jehovah, Allah, *Ishwara, Jagadamba,* and by many other names. Universal truths, similarly, are the same everywhere. Religion is no mere ornament of civilization: It is the fundamental need of all human beings. Rightly understood, true religion offers hope and inspiration impartially. Its forms vary with different cultures and different social conditioning, but always its purpose is to raise human consciousness. Truth never endorses any one culture exclusively. People who seek truth earnestly find their understanding becoming ever-increasingly refined.

What I have written so far, then, is not a plea for syncretism. It is not, in other words, a proposal to compromise true teachings for the sake of establishing interreligious harmony. Only in higher awareness, never in compromise, can the universality of truth become generally accepted. Oneness must be *experienced,* not merely proclaimed. It is not something society can vote into existence.

Here, then, is the purpose of this book: to encourage people everywhere to seek a *meaningful* relationship with God, and to establish, as a projection of that inner relationship, the brotherhood of all mankind. The noble plant, truth, will never flourish except in the soil of spiritual love. In desert wastes of dogmatism and sectarian rivalries it can only, as history demonstrates, wither and die. When the plant is nourished by "living waters" of selfless love—to paraphrase the words of Jesus Christ—it will suffice for every human need.

The religions of the world are only denominations in the one, universal religion, Truth. The classifications of Hinduism, Buddhism, Christianity, Islam, and all the others are superficial, despite every claim to the contrary. True religion merits the indigenous name for religion in India: *Sanaatan Dharma,* "the Eternal Religion," or, more exactly, "The Way to Eternal Enlightenment."* Insofar as evidence is actually available, sectarianism is itself a soap

Dharma means "religion, or way," which implies movement or development of some kind. *Sanaatan* ("eternal"), however, implies eternal truth–that which exists beyond time and space. I therefore prefer to render the term, *Sanaatan Dharma,* as "The Way to Eternal Enlightenment," and not the standard English rendering, "The Eternal Religion." For implied in the term is the eternity of enlightenment, and *not* some one and only (to those who are addicted to sectarian beliefs), "eternal way."

bubble: colorful, perhaps, but lacking in substance. For want of evidence, people with sectarian attitudes advance their claims with emotional fervor. Facts would give their reasoning powers something to "chew on," but unsubstantiated claims usually distort truth, even as bubbles do the images reflected in them. Truth alone transcends the limitations of human understanding.

Belief is hypothesis; faith, on the other hand, is born of experience. In the evolution of thought, conditioned as we've become by scientific methodology, it is time we focused on the actual experience of spiritual truth, and on the wisdom brought by that experience. It is time all men recognized as superstition the separatist, but unsubstantiated, claims so long prevalent in orthodox religion.

Faith is wisdom. And wisdom is the awareness of man's relationship to Cosmic Verity.

The term, Hinduism, was a foreign imposition on the religious system of India, based on the scholarship of Westerners. This long-accepted view was reported by John Garrett in *A Classical Dictionary of India* in 1871, who wrote that "a people who spoke Sanskrit, and followed the religion of the Vedas, came into India in some very distant age from lands west of the Indus." This view of history is coming under increasing scrutiny by modern scholars, more and more of whom reject it as false. Indian indigenous tradition gives no hint of such a view.

CHAPTER TWO

A Brief History of Religion

What can inspire the followers of the world's different religions to see one another as fellow members in one family of Truth, with God, their Father/Mother, at the head? The beauty of this concept is surely self-evident to every thoughtful person. Its realization, however, may also appear to them, given historical precedents, impossible.

Buddha might seem to have been sanctioning sectarianism when he urged people not to depend on the Vedic gods and rituals.* His disciples thought his meaning was that he didn't believe in God. In fact, he was seeking only to correct their misunderstanding of the scriptures. They took his message entirely as a doctrine of self-reliance, which to them meant the exclusion of any need for God. Thus, Buddhism evolved as an atheistic religion.

---

*The Vedas are the ancient, sacred books of Hinduism. "Vedic" is the adjective.

What Buddha wanted was to encourage people to take spiritual responsibility for their own lives, and not to depend passively on God, or on minor "gods," for boons of temporary fulfillment. The fact that Buddha never said not to pray—indeed, Buddhists themselves pray to the Buddha—makes it clear that he didn't exclude divine grace: He simply emphasized the importance of personal effort in addition to faith in God.

Swami Shankaracharya, centuries later, corrected this imbalance. It wasn't Buddha's teachings he contested, but only people's misconceptions concerning them. God, he explained, is pure Spirit beyond all duality. That Supreme Spirit is the only reality in existence. Shankaracharya — Shankara, as he is also known—taught that the goal of life is union with the Absolute, which he described as *Satchidananda:* Existence (*Sat*), Consciousness (*Chid*), Bliss (*Ananda*). *Advaitins*—believers in *advaita,** or non-dualism — later took his teaching not only as his reply to Buddhism, but as his definition of Hinduism itself. Nothing, they proclaimed, exists except that Absolute; all else is delusion. And since, by their understanding,

*A combination of two words: "*a*," meaning "non," and "*dwaita*," or "duality." The "w" in *advaita* is more correct, but is less commonly used.

manifested creation is only a dream, it doesn't even exist.

Here was another of the misconceptions that surface repeatedly in religion. For dreams do, of course, exist — *as dreams!* If a person hits his head in a dream, his dream head will hurt. Creation, in other words, does exist in its own context. It simply isn't what it appears to be.

The problem with Buddhism as the Buddhists presented it was that it admitted of nothing toward which love and devotion could be directed. Without love, spiritual progress is ineffectual, like a man on crutches in a race against Olympic athletes.

The problem with *advaita,* on the other hand, as Shankaracharya's successors presented it, was comparable. They admitted of no one *by whom* devotion could be directed. In this concept, again, there was no place for love. Since only the Absolute exists, duality cannot exist. Who, then, can be devoted to whom? If the ego is a delusion, human love itself must be a delusion also, since it implies the duality of subject and object, lover and beloved. Overlooked in their reasoning was that Shankaracharya *himself* had composed devotional hymns to God as the Divine Mother. Hindus quote a verse from a song of his: "Bad sons there are many, but never a bad Mother!"

Ramanuja tried centuries later to correct this flaw in *advaitic* reasoning. He taught a devotional form of *advaita* known as *Vishishta-Advaita*. The soul itself, he declared, is not a delusion, but exists eternally. It can, and must, develop a relationship of love with the Creator.

The great masters have never opposed one another's teachings. Truth, after all, is both universal and eternal. It never changes. Scientific discoveries, accepted by many as finalities, lose their "finality" every few years, as new facts come to light. The masters, by contrast, have realized the eternal, forever unchanging truth. That is what they declare in every age and every religion. Their mission is to correct people's misunderstandings of the truth. Because human beings are habitually restless, they feel attracted to complexity and shun divine simplicity. They embellish with ego-gratifying variations the pristine melodies of the soul.

Another illustration may help: If the goal is to go to the equator, those living in the Northern Hemisphere will be instructed to go south. Those, on the other hand, who live in the Southern Hemisphere will be told to go north. Those traveling southward, having been so instructed, will probably — considering usual human behavior — continue in that direction after they've reached the equator. When they encounter others in the Southern Hemisphere, moving northward, they cry, "No! No! you're supposed to go *south!*" Thus arise sectarian differences, which are the curse of religion everywhere.

Chaitanya, centuries after Ramanuja, emphasized the importance of devotion. He was already famous as a brilliant scholar when a dramatic vision of Krishna changed his life. After that transformation, he began urging people to abandon philosophical speculation as dry and profitless — he himself was expert at such speculation — and to immerse themselves in the love of God. It is, he said, useless to try to *define* God: the very attempt merely leads the mind into an arid wasteland of intellectual theories. Man needs nothing except God's *love*. Chaitanya taught people to worship the Lord by chanting to Him devotedly in the form of Krishna.

His teaching by no means contradicted the non-dualism of Swami Shankaracharya, even if it seemed to. Rather, he urged people to accept, and be true to, their own *actual* state of consciousness.

"*Harer nam, Harer nam, Harer nam* **kevalyam!** — the Lord's name, the Lord's name, **the Lord's name** is man's *only* path to salvation!" This was his famous declaration. Many of his followers —

Vaishnavas, they are called — took his teaching literally and insisted that Krishna himself *is* the Lord. The truth, of course, is quite the opposite; this was their special error. Krishna, the man, could not possibly be God. God, rather, is Krishna; God is *all* His manifestations. The wave is not the ocean. On the contrary: the ocean has become all of its waves. It is a fallacy to claim that any one wave can be the whole ocean! Christians have made this same mistake regarding Jesus Christ.

Images of Krishna symbolize a number of deep truths. Vaishnavas, however, have accepted those symbols as the truth itself. Because tradition depicted Krishna as blue-skinned, for example, Vaishnavas say his skin was therefore actually blue. His traditional coloring is, in fact, symbolic of the sky, which in turn is a symbol for infinity. God, in other words, is infinite. Indeed, He is also *nirakara,* or formless. To visualize Him thus, however, is difficult for most people, who are accustomed to substantial, material realities. Hence this metaphorical portrayal.

Tradition shows Krishna playing the flute. This, too, is symbolic; it is a reference to God's inner call to the soul to "dance" with Him in cosmic bliss. There is, indeed, a further explanation for his flute. For sometimes in meditation, when the mind is interiorized, a flute-like sound is heard in the inner ear. The yoga teachings explain that this sound appears when the body's energy is relaxed and centered in the spine. This book is not the place, however, for an extended explanation of those esoteric teachings.

The Krishna legend, like numerous other Hindu writings, abounds with symbolism. They are meant to stir the heart with devotion rather than instruct the mind in theology. The spiritually immature need steps to climb as they ascend toward wisdom. In this sense, most people are like those little girls playing with dolls and in the process preparing themselves, inadvertently, for future motherhood.

Chaitanya's very exhortation to chant the name of God had also a deeper meaning. It was suggested by his own frequent states of breathless ecstasy, in which all mental activity, including mental chanting and prayer, ceases. Silent communion ensues then, and God's actual name is heard: AUM, the vibratory sound of all creation. This saving name cannot be uttered by human lips.

The Vaishnavas have dogmatically denounced *advaita*. Even today, they consider the two paths incompatible. In fact, however, both are facets of the one diamond of Truth, each valid in its context and on its own level of application. Man imagines himself capable of comprehending all things with the intellect alone. In this presumption he is like a little child whom St. Augustine, the great Christian theologian, beheld on a beach.

The child was trying to empty the sea by filling his little bucket with sea water, then emptying it repeatedly onto the sand. According to legend, St. Augustine asked the child, "Isn't it foolish to try to empty the sea with that little bucket?" The child gazed up at him calmly and replied, "And isn't it foolish to try to empty the sea of divine wisdom with the 'bucket' of your little mind?" Having said those words, the child vanished!

Indians were charitable enough in their spiritual consciousness to absorb such divergent beliefs without growing confused as to their longing for God. Such is the genius of that great civilization! Unfortunately, even in that country religion has brought disunity, for which blame is due to human ignorance, not to religion itself. The Indians' hunger for truth remained, but alas, so also did bigotry. A person's ignorance is usually displayed in the subjects that interest him, not in those to which he is indifferent. Westerners, many of whom scorn Hinduism as "superstitious," are often, themselves, lukewarm to religious truths. The fact is, few people anywhere are spiritually mature. The great masters have had repeatedly to explain those aspects of the truth for which mankind has had a special need.

In Palestine, another great master, Moses, taught people to worship one God instead of many gods. In this respect his teachings were like Buddha's. Both masters insisted on self-ef-fort and right action. And both spoke against the worship of lesser deities—angels as they are called in Christian tradition—in the hope of re-ceiving wealth, pleasure, success, and worldly power in recompense. Moses again, like Bud-dha, urged people to develop their own inner strength, and to shun all lesser goals as ulti-mately disillusioning. He taught people to love the Supreme Lord, and to obey His command-ments faithfully.

In the centuries following Moses, the Jews, with considerable ingenuity, developed endless ramifications of the Law of Moses. They forgot his supreme commandment, to love God with one's whole heart, and to love everyone in God's name. Instead, they fell away gradually from devotion to God, and became engrossed in religious technicalities. Such always is the danger, when the priesthood of a religion gains too firm a hold on guiding it: Minor details— important to professionals in every field—take precedence over the spontaneous expression of love. Again and again, the prophets sought to guide the Jewish people back to a closer relationship with the Lord. Alas! again and again the Jews returned to their legalisms. They even went so far as to persecute their prophets, whose only desire was to help them. How sad, that humanity should reciprocate love with hatred! The truths taught by the great masters have the power to change lives and bestow on all the fulfillment they want from life. Unenlightened humanity, alas! prefers to wallow, buffalo-like, in the mud of its delusions, and rejects the divine call to the path of true, inner freedom.

The age-old emphasis in the East has been on man's *individual* relationship with truth and with God. In the West, the emphasis has been on society, and on people's relationship as a whole to reality. This difference is observable at every level. In music, for example, the melodies of Indian music suggest deep, personal longing for God. That music contrasts sharply with the intricate instrumental patterns and rich harmonies of Western music, where chord progressions suggest a crowd of people gathered together to express group feelings and group intentions.

It is time that these diverse emphases were

united in one compatible whole. Social evolution needs to be balanced, now, with individual development.

What Jesus Christ taught was not a contradiction of the Mosaic Law but, as he himself stated, its *fulfillment*. He stressed the supreme importance of *loving* God. Western emphasis on group consciousness, however, soon changed what was an essentially Eastern approach to truth, bringing his teachings under the control of a central organization. In exercising this control, the church diluted Christ's message, developing an essentially outward focus. Herein lay its own special misunderstanding of the truth. Christianity, too, needs to balance its understanding of truth: to bring organizational control into harmony with individual conscience.

Mohammed, several centuries later, was born among peoples less inclined to the meditative life. He sought to accomplish what Moses had done: Instead of many gods, he told people to worship one God, Allah. His allegiance was to "The Book"—that is to say, to The Holy Bible. His hope was to unite all those of "The Book" into a single faith. Jews and Christians repudiated the claim of Moslems that Mohammed had introduced a new revelation. Warfare between Christians and Moslems was the consequence. And sectarianism, already rampant in the West, became inflamed in the Semitic branch of religion. The conflict between this branch and that deriving from Hinduism—Buddhism, Jainism, and Sikhism—obscured still further any likelihood that man would ever accept that the divine truth is basically one.

Many people today are doubtful whether religion, as a civilized activity, will ever be influential in creating peace and harmony on earth. Must it remain always, then, a source of conflict? If man is to grow in wisdom—not to speak of not bombing himself out of existence!—it is important that a new understanding dawn in human hearts.

Modern science, dedicated though it is to merely material goals, has come closer to universal agreement than religion ever has. Scientific proofs in Bangkok, Tokyo, or Jakarta are not scorned by scientists elsewhere as "foreign." Science bases its quest on experimentation, not on *a priori* beliefs. Many people today, impressed by the proofs of science, conclude that only materially demonstrable facts are worthy of investigation. Moral values, to them, are therefore valid in only a relative sense. This is to say that such values are subjectively valid, but not universally so. Life itself, people claim, is bereft of meaning. Some even carry this thought to the extent of insisting that morality is whatever a person wants it to be. The important thing only is that he be true to himself. Widespread confusion has resulted from this reasoning. People overlook that the principles of behavior, like religious truths, are not rooted in opinion but in natural law.

One of the basic functions of religion is to provide solutions to the moral and spiritual dilemmas of mankind. Unfortunately, what institutional religion has too often done is fan the flames; sometimes, it has even ignited them! Buddhists' insistence that only the Buddha can grant release from the wheel of rebirth is not welcomed kindly by people who seek their salvation through Jesus Christ, or through Krishna. Hindus squabble endlessly over the distinctions of *dwaita, advaita, vishishta-advaita, vaishnavism,* and the worship of God as the Divine Mother. Moslems claim that Mohammed is the prophet of Allah. Christians insist that Jesus Christ is the "only way." Christians also condemn the "pantheistic" teachings of Hinduism as animistic, and believe, erroneously, that Hindu deities are the "idols" against which Moses inveighed so sternly. What Moses was warning against, in fact, were the "idols" of material desire. The Hindu deities have always represented not materialistic goals, but spiritual *principles.*

Is there any hope for peace in this tumult of contradictions? Indeed there is! The hope for religion lies in religious history itself—not in its lamentable squabbles, but in the repeated efforts of great masters to return mankind to the underlying, eternal purpose of religion. Theirs is not the fuzzy broad-mindedness of people who are indifferent to, and consequently myopic regarding, spiritual truths. It is the clear focus of men and women of divine wisdom.

The great Moslem woman saint, Rabbi'a, once said, "He is no true lover of God who does not forget his suffering in the contemplation of the Divine Beloved." The message of every great master is the same: "Forget your sorrow-producing conflicts: Love God!"

The further purpose of this book, then, is to show convincingly that behind every great scripture in the world lies the wisdom of eternity.

CHAPTER THREE

The Goal of Life

The oldest and surest method of learning is that of punishment and reward. A child is scolded or punished if he does something wrong, and praised or rewarded for doing something well. Rats can be trained to follow preselected paths through a maze by giving them a mild electric shock if they choose wrongly, and placing a tasty morsel at the end of the right choice. Even worms have been reported to learn by these methods.

The model for this kind of training lies in Nature herself. The pain one experiences if one goes against Nature, and the pleasure if one co-operates with it, is one way all creatures are guided—not always infallibly, but in a general sense correctly. A child learns, if it touches a hot stove, not to repeat the experiment. Sensitivity to extreme heat is given us for our protection, not for our misery. All living creatures learn, quickly or slowly according to their intelligence, what "works" for them and what doesn't.

If a child plunders the cookie jar, it may learn from repeated forays that too many cookies give tummy aches. Meanwhile, he may be helped by a stern reprimand, but experience itself, if not too drastic, is always the best teacher.

As creatures learn to avoid pain and to seek pleasure, so man strives to avoid also mental suffering and to seek happiness. Punishment and reward encourage life in the long process of evolution from the lowly germ to the spiritual enlightenment of masters like Jesus Christ and Buddha. At life's higher stages of development, man's twofold desire to avoid suffering and find happiness becomes refined to an intense desire for escape from ego-bondage and a companion desire for expansion in spiritual bliss.

Consciousness and bliss are one and the same, and are the underlying reality of existence. Conscious bliss is the essential reality behind every soaring cloud, firm rock, flowing river, and oxygen-giving tree, and behind moving and breathing creatures everywhere. Science errs in saying that everything is essentially without consciousness. Its error is due to the fact that it began its journey of discovery with an inquiry into mechanisms. "How?" it asked, discounting the further questions, "What?" and "Why?" The "how" of things explains their mechanisms. The further questions, "what" and "why," pertain to motivation. These questions will be addressed in the following pages.

Consciousness and bliss are *innate* in everything. The very universe was manifested out of Absolute Spirit: ever-conscious, ever-existing, *ever-new* Bliss, or *Satchidananda* as Swami Shankaracharya called it.

Evolution is driven by the impulse in all creatures to avoid threats to their own bliss-potential. What each one perceives of that potential depends on its own level of evolution. To the more primitive creatures it may mean only comfort; to others, food. Nevertheless, according to the degree of awareness expressed in each one, it is bliss they seek. Therefore, the loss of bliss is what they try to avoid.

Charles Darwin declared that survival is the primary impulse of life. This instinct, however, is no mindless urge. If creatures struggle *consciously* to maintain their existence, it is because, to them, it represents something important. They cling to it not as a mere projection of Newtonian inertia. Rather, they cling because their awareness is a manifestation, however inchoate, of bliss. Survival is a paramount concern for them only when their lives are actively threatened, for they want to preserve their present measure of conscious bliss. Otherwise, all they want is simply to enjoy life.

Bliss is heavily veiled in the lower forms of life. The highest to which they aspire is to avoid physical pain, and to experience physical pleasure. Man is different in that his aspiration is more deliberate, and more personal. With his relatively refined awareness, he realizes also that physical sensations are usually brief in duration, and that the emotional ups and downs that accompany pleasure and pain are temporary, like tossing ocean waves. Thus, he envisions something more permanent than pleasure, and seeks happiness. He tries to avoid mental suffering also—the loss of a job, for instance, or of reputation—and willingly endures even physical pain to achieve long-range goals. With further refinement of his awareness, he seeks to avoid feelings, thoughts, and actions that might prevent him from realizing eternal bliss. For he has discovered that the source of all suffering lies in the fact that his attention has been diverted from his own reality.

Happiness springs from within the self. It doesn't depend on outer conditions. Nothing outside ourselves, therefore, can define or qualify our happiness except as we allow it to do so. Once this unalterable truth is realized, happiness become our permanent possession.

Unfortunately, life conditions people to seek

fulfillment outside, not inside, themselves. As energy forms the body in the womb, it conditions the fetus, and later on the newborn baby, to seek expression outwardly also. The baby needs milk. It must work at developing its body's movements. Life itself is an adventure in learning how to relate to objective reality. Gradually, the adventure becomes one of learning to discriminate between what is real what merely seems so.

The world as the senses present it to us is a mirage. It seems hard or soft to the touch; pleasant or unpleasant to the palate; beautiful or ugly to the eyes; harmonious or cacophonous to the ears; sweet or acrid to the sense of smell. In fact, it is none of these things. Clues are given us to a very different reality. Solid-seeming matter can be penetrated by sound waves, and by x-rays. Food that human beings abominate is eagerly ingested by other creatures. The senses constantly deceive us, for they expose us to a very limited range of sound and light vibrations. What seems to us pleasant or unpleasant is often a very subjective evaluation, widely varied even within the narrow "spectrum" of human tastes. "Beauty," it is said, "is in the eye of the beholder." The eye can be trained to see beauty everywhere. People can also be conditioned by disappointment to see ugliness everywhere, as they sow their experiences as seeds of further unhappiness.

We refer things back constantly to our *reactions*, without which objective reality would hold little meaning for us. People realize in time that their most intimate reality is their own state of consciousness. It is in their reactions that they suffer or rejoice. One's reactions should therefore be his paramount concern.

What is man, relative to the vast universe? Is he utterly insignificant, as the findings of astronomy might suggest? We see ourselves instinctively as central to everything in existence. Nor is this instinct misguided. For it is our own perception that must expand. In ourselves also, our perceptions can shrink. Life leads us by expanding sympathy to an ever-more refined awareness. It also, if we allow it to, leads us to a contracting sympathy, and a gradually diminishing awareness, by which our potential for bliss is suppressed.

Pain and pleasure are our first teachers. The pain causes us to contract inwardly—not mentally only, but in physical tension. Pleasure brings a feeling of relaxation and mental expansion. We gradually learn to associate suffering more with mental than with physical tension, and happiness more with mental well-being.

From these facts it emerges that moral principles have their roots in Nature. Why is it wrong to steal from others, or to injure them? Not because of societal or scriptural strictures, but because one is punished by his own nature, which causes physical contraction and tension, and a mentally self-defensive attitude. To go against natural law is to offend against ourselves. As a consequence, we experience pain. Thus, even if the pirate who robs others views himself as the gainer, materially speaking, his contraction of sympathy and his accompanying fear of retribution is a constant punishment for disturbing the harmony in himself and in his surroundings. The very universe becomes, for him, a hostile environment. Increasing inner disharmony becomes at last intolerable to him in the alienation it brings him from others, and, despite every affirmation to the contrary, in his diminishing sense of self-worth.

Growth in understanding can be accomplished only by the *individual.* Of what use to a child the reassurances that others, some day, will become adults? Evolution itself is not focused so much on developing new species as it is on the progress of individual awareness. Society may have to restrain its members if they persist in anti-social behavior, but the laws of human nature exact their own price, ultimately.

The wrongdoer eventually punishes himself. Foolish is he who scoffs, "Oh, *eventually!* Who cares about 'eventually'?" Eventually, however, will be very much *right now,* when it arrives!

Spiritual evolution causes man, in addition to animal concerns with physical pain and pleasure, an awareness also of mental punishment and reward. As his refinement increases, he seeks to avoid mental suffering, and to find happiness in an uplifted state of mind.

These are, however, subtle lessons. Time is required, usually, for even one of them to be learned well. The span of one lifetime is too short for very much to be accomplished in the way of self-development. The long evolutionary process cannot be drastically curtailed — producing, let us say, enlightened worms! Enlightenment, moreover, which is an *inner awakening,* cannot be achieved *outwardly* by manifesting a perfect species, as opposed to manifesting individual perfection.

Here, ineluctably, arises the question of reincarnation. For without many lifetimes in which to learn and grow, it would be impossible for there to be a meaningful process of evolution. Evolution toward complexity? Yes, of course. This exists already. But complexity in itself is not a proof of *progress.* What evolution manifests also is growing awareness in life's manifestations. For that reason alone evolution is progressive. Otherwise it could only be considered *progressive change*. What is expressed in life, and in the universe, however, is consciousness. Progress can be considered such only if it is toward a perfect expression of *consciousness*. Outer, material perfection in this realm of relativities is a contradiction in terms. Perfection cannot be even visualized, except in terms of individual development.

Reincarnation is, at present, a controversial subject: not one to be resolved dogmatically by scriptural quotations, any more than the concepts of God could be resolved that we discussed earlier. In the past, claims that lacked the support of sensory evidence were justified simply by quoting the scriptures. Materialists, of course, scoffed at them, but they were in the minority, or else remained prudently silent. Science today has brought materialism into the open, but has shown convincingly that countless phenomena exist beyond sensory awareness: the atom and the electron, for example; invisible radio waves; the fact that "solid" matter consists mostly of space. Most of the claims of modern science have become acceptable not because common sense endorses them, but *because they have produced results*.

The results, similarly, of the doctrine of reincarnation give it so much convincing support that reason, confronted by them, rejects any other explanation. Reasonable premises may not always receive outward endorsement, but the universe has never shown itself *un*reasonable.

What coherent meaning, indeed, can be discerned in life without a continuity of *individual* awareness? If a human being begins life with a blank slate, giving no sign of any previous experience, how much can he be expected realistically to learn in his brief life span? A child in kindergarten cannot be expected to learn advanced physics: He must go through many years of training first. How much *more* time, then, is required for developing wisdom! Deep insight is not the product of cleverness. Nor is it necessarily a sign of keen intelligence. It is the product of long-pondered, personal experience.

Rationalizations to the contrary notwithstanding, someone who is born into a criminal environment, and killed in a gang war before reaching the age of twenty, has neither the opportunity nor, probably, the incentive to absorb life's higher lessons.

The people we see around us, perhaps daily, live quite obviously on many different levels of development. Often it takes a mere glance at their expressions to perceive that all of them are not equally wise. The differences suggest powerfully that all human beings are in a process of development — not as a species merely, *but as individuals.* A single lifetime may not suffice to absorb *even one* basic lesson of life: the superior rewards, for instance, of kindness over callousness, and of generosity over selfishness. Nor is one lifetime sufficient to free one from *even one* powerful bad habit, such as alcoholism or drug addiction. Strong habits grow deep roots in the subconscious mind. They wind unseen through subterranean caverns of memory, crisscrossed with tunnels of ancient self-justification, hurt, and unresolved disappointment.

The motivation that drives everyone, including the lower animals, is desire. All seek to avoid pain and experience pleasure. The tiger, in seeking to satisfy its own hunger, evinces no pity for its prey. Human "tigers," similarly, can be pitiless toward those whom they destroy in their ambition for self-aggrandizement. Cruelty may be as natural to persons like them as it is to tigers. They may require lifetimes of suffering before their nature can be refined to, let us say, one of loving compassion.

Human beings are more developed in intelligence and understanding than other animals.

Consequently they soon discover how temporary life's physical and emotional sensations are. Today's pleasure, or pain, may be only a memory by tomorrow. Humanity is therefore inclined to seek fulfillment of a more permanent kind. Most people want happiness, which is a state of mental well-being. Because even they, however, are still evolving toward wisdom (the process is by no means automatic, for it is influenced by free will), most people, even if they want happiness, identify it erroneously with outer, tangible gains. They identify permanence with possessions. Thus, their search for happiness is diverted.

Consider a typical detour: A person is strolling down the street without a care in the world. The day is beautiful; birds sing melodiously in the trees; the sun is shining brightly in a lightly clouded sky. A gentle breeze wafts the scent of lilacs, fresh-sprinkled with the dew, from a nearby garden. The man thinks, "How perfectly wonderful life is!"

All at once, perched on a tree limb just above his head, he spies a gay-colored bird framed gracefully by surrounding branches. Soft clouds form the backdrop to this scene, sailing like majestic galleons through the blue sky.

"If only I had a camera!" the man thinks. "I

could catch this image on film and have it with me forever!" That passing happiness has suddenly awakened in him a desire for something more permanent: a material possession.

Alas! poor fellow, he can't afford a camera! What can he do? This desire is too sudden to be deep, but even so its ripples dance on the surface of his heart. "If only I had a camera!" he repeats. "Ah, *if only!* How many other pictures I could then take and keep with me forever."

Somehow, the sunlight no longer seems to him quite so brilliant. The birds' songs no longer thrill him so deeply. His feelings churn with schemes for how he can afford to buy that camera.

From now on he scrimps and saves. Months pass. The strength of this desire grows. At last he finds he can fulfill the desire. Meanwhile, he has carefully researched the market, and one particular model has caught his fancy.

Now then, what about those happy walks down the street that set him on this mental journey of exploration? He hasn't had time for them. Ah well, never mind: Now he has, as his very own, the camera of his dreams. What joy is his!

Or is it? Here is an interesting point to consider: He was happy *before* his decision that he wanted that camera. Today, with his new acquisition in hand, *is he any happier?* Oh, yes, he is more *excited,* but is he any *happier?* Wasn't his happiness that day due partly to the calmness of his enjoyment? Can he sincerely equate this excitement with that moment of unconditioned happiness? The truth is, his present happiness, compared to what he had before, is an uncomfortable compromise.

For his joy now is centered *outside* himself. No longer does it well up from a sense of *inner* well-being. All he has accomplished is *remove* the condition he placed on his happiness by telling himself he needed a camera for happiness to be complete. How much, beyond that, has he achieved? He owns the camera, and its possession seems the happy ending to a great adventure. Still, ...

Dare we ask? How long will this "happy ending" endure? Only as long, surely, as it takes him to balance out the intensity of that desire, and the difficulty of fulfilling it, with his feeling of having grown used to his possession. After a time, he finds that he needs to re-affirm his happiness. He may gather friends about him and regale them with his "Saga of the Camera," repeating again and again what a stroke of luck it was to be able to get it. He explains the research it took, and why this model so ideally suits his needs. Finally, with a triumphant air, he displays his best photos.

The time must arrive during this process when he notices in himself a certain let-down. The problem is, his new camera is no longer new! In fact, it is beginning to seem a bit "old hat." Rarely, now, does he feel that joyful lift of initial possession. Even the compliments people pay him no longer mean much to him.

His desire for a camera has, it may now be said, been well and truly fulfilled. Wouldn't one think he'd return, now, to strolling down the street and enjoying the birds' songs and the flowers fresh-sprinkled with the dew? For some reason, he just doesn't. He asks himself instead, "What new object can I possess?" He has seen telephoto lenses, wide-angle lenses, and countless other useful attachments for his camera. Should he get one of those? The satisfaction of one desire has set in motion a tendency in him to continue to seek happiness by fulfilling other desires: ten of them—a hundred—a thousand! The more he seeks happiness in outer fulfillment, the more he finds himself entangled in the process itself. No longer is he able to live in the present. Desire keeps him living in the future—a future that forever recedes.

Was he not actually happier that first day, strolling cheerfully down the street? This camera was supposed to increase his happiness;

instead, it has made him focus outside himself for his fulfillment. Yet happiness on that occasion was already his!

Rich people for this reason are often dissatisfied with life. Others, less wealthy than they though able to satisfy their basic needs, may in fact be much happier. For the rich it is so easy to fulfill every whim—and so difficult to be contented in the fulfillment! Countless desires jostle about in their hearts, each of them insisting on being given priority attention. How can the poor rich person decide which of his clamorous desires to fulfill first? Little wonder statistics show proportionately more suicides among the rich than among the poor.

Happiness simply does not exist in things. As gifts are wrapped prior to being given in order to make them more alluring, so people enclose their desires in colorful "wrapping" of alluring expectations. Imagination can surround even the most common object with an attractive glow. The fulfillment promised, however, is in itself empty—like the tin cans that are offered for purchase by tourists that proclaim: "Air from Capri, Italy!" or, "Air from Yosemite Valley." The cans are empty, of course. Mere things, like them, are all empty, themselves, of any actual power to satisfy! We may label them mentally, "Happiness," but all we do is project the thought of happiness onto them. When we direct our expectations outward, away from ourselves, imagination can take us as far from the actual source of happiness as it is capable of soaring.

This is not to say that all desires must be abandoned. As well might one try to live without breathing! It is possible, however, to lessen the grip of one's *attachment* to those desires. Non-attachment, not non-possession, is the secret of happiness. Wealthy people, too, who learn this lesson can be perfectly happy!

Everyone needs above all to learn that material desires are merely expressions of soul-longing for our native state: Eternal Bliss. This longing can be fulfilled only in one's self. That person strolling carefree down the street may have been better off at that moment than he has ever been since then, despite his later delight in acquiring a camera.

It is wise, therefore, when desiring material possessions, never to accept the thought that one cannot live without them. Material ends should be sought in a spirit of inner freedom, by constantly affirming bliss *within*.

This practice is relatively easy if one keeps an attitude of non-attachment. This does not mean one should be apathetic or indifferent. Without inner freedom it is never really possible to enjoy anything. Non-attachment is, indeed, the path to inner freedom.

Refer every enjoyment, therefore, back to your inner bliss. If you have not experienced bliss, recall a time of happiness in your life and use that as an aid in visualizing the soul-bliss within.

The freedom of non-attachment itself is a signpost to inner bliss.

CHAPTER FOUR

Pleasure Is Counterfeit Happiness

Happiness is, for most human beings, the goal of life, more so even than pleasure. Pleasure is dependent on the senses, and is therefore primarily physical in origin. Good food is an example. We don't think of the lower animals as having the capacity for actual happiness. A strong-willed person can manage to be happy *in spite of* adverse conditions, but a dog isn't likely to wag its tail bravely in the face of hunger and misfortune.

As we contemplate the progression of consciousness toward its apotheosis in bliss, it is important to distinguish between pleasure and happiness. Pleasure is false happiness, even though people commonly treat them as meaning more or less the same thing. The expression, "happy as a clam," comes from someone's notion that clams are without worries and must therefore be happy. A worry-free existence is not necessarily, however, a happy one. Bliss, at a clam's level of evolution, is veiled, as I said earlier. It is unlikely to be more than a vague feeling of comfort, perhaps when consuming food.

To be able to feel actual pleasure requires a higher degree of awareness. Higher animals—the vertebrates in particular—are obviously more capable than the clam of enjoying life. They take pleasure in many activities besides those needed for survival. Gazelles, as they leap through the long grasses of an African veldt, obviously delight in doing so. Birds sing not only to attract mates—as people who focus on survival as the sole explanation for evolution might insist—but because they *enjoy* singing. Mates wouldn't be attracted to them, moreover, if they too didn't enjoy *listening*. Pleasure, then, is a stage well above the clam in the evolution of consciousness toward bliss.

And happiness is a stage above pleasure. Both happiness and pleasure are responses of the mind, but pleasure requires sensory stimulation, whereas happiness is self-generated. A person's delight in a summer day indicates *both* pleasure *and* happiness: pleasure, in his response to the weather and the beautiful scenery; happiness, in his self-awareness. Happiness depends on nothing external to oneself: It is generated by an act of will.

The happiness of that man we saw strolling

down the street in the last chapter, before he conceived a desire for a camera, needn't have been the consequence of the sunlight and the birds singing. I gave that scene a pleasant setting only as a poetic device, to emphasize how the man felt, inwardly. But if he was truly happy, his happiness wouldn't actually have depended on anything outside himself.

Otherwise, it would have been merely a good mood, lacking in substance. Moods, like pleasure, are dependent on the senses and are as changeable as the weather. The little-known cause of moodiness, in fact, is overindulgence in sense pleasures — if not recently, then at some time in the past.

In telling that story I wasn't trying to show the man in a good mood. I wanted to distinguish between happiness and the restrictions placed on it by desire. In the present context my aim is to distinguish between self-generated happiness and outwardly dependent pleasure. Were I retelling the story here, I might describe the man as ill, afflicted with arthritic pain, and slogging through deep mud on a winter night, yet happy just the same. With a strong will, he'd have been able to ignore every difficulty; his happiness would have remained unaffected. I don't mean those circumstances would have been *pleasurable*. I mean only that a human being can be happy under the worst circumstances. Conditions, in fact, are always neutral; they seem happy or sad owing only to the attitudes of the mind.

There is a story in India about a devotee of God named Haridas, a companion of Chaitanya (whom I mentioned in Chapter Two). Haridas was born a Moslem. He grew up, however, to love God in the Hindu form of Krishna, having been inspired to that love by Chaitanya. He then took the name *Haridas,* to indicate a servant of Krishna in the aspect of Hari, the "thief of hearts." The king of that region, a Moslem, was outraged at Haridas's apostasy, and ordered him to recant. Haridas refused. The king then condemned him to death by flogging.

His executioners suspended him by his wrists from a tree. As they were tying him up, Haridas prayed, "Lord Krishna, my Beloved, bless them that they, too, feel Thy love!"

The executioners began to beat him mercilessly with cudgels. Haridas, however, felt nothing for them but love. So magnetic was his expanding joy that the crowd, gathered there to witness the execution, began to feel uplifted by it. One by one they were caught up in joy, until all were dancing in a kind of ecstasy. The executioners, at last overcome also, let their cudgels fall to the ground and joined in, dancing in devotional joy.

Such joy, certainly, cannot be produced by mere mental resolution. It is an extraordinary act of grace. No attitude alone could *manufacture* even the happiness we are discussing here. Our discussion here, however, concerns the stages on the way to divine bliss. Bliss, being conscious, filters down into human consciousness when the mind is held open to receive it. The very affirmation of happiness is what opens the mind. Add to it devotion and faith, and the heart's doors are opened wide to receive divine states of consciousness.

There is another story, this one of Western origin. Benvenuto Cellini, the Italian artist of Renaissance times, wrote in his autobiography of a difference of opinion he'd once had with the pope. The pope wanted him to work on a new project. Cellini wanted payment for the last project. Power resided with the pope, however, who had him cast into a dungeon to reconsider his priorities.

The artist in his autobiography described the conditions in that dungeon: a damp mattress, a cold cell, rats running about freely, and only enough light from a high window to permit him to read for one hour a day. He had a copy of The Holy Bible with him, and read from it every day for that hour. The rest of his waking moments, he prayed.

Cellini was a stubborn man, and refused to succumb to these obviously adverse conditions. His positive attitude, combined with his faith, brought him gradually such upliftment of consciousness that he wrote later, "If you want to know what true happiness is, arrange to be thrown into a dungeon. Ask for a damp mattress [and he went on to describe the material setting he'd known], and spend your waking moments praying to God."

Cellini, I should add, was finally released by the pope, who agreed to pay him for his past services!

It is, then, possible to enjoy life under the direst conditions. For life itself is a crucible of bliss. We cannot receive bliss passively, however. Our consciousness must be kept in a fit frame of mind to receive it. Above all, we must be determined to be inwardly happy. It takes a strong will to hold firmly to it. It takes a strong will also to remain inwardly calm under trying circumstances. Without calmness, however, the flow of bliss would quickly diminish to a trickle. It should be clear, then, that happiness is positive, never passive, as bliss itself is positive. One cannot be happy by mere wishful thinking.

Pleasure, on the other hand, is a mental *re-*

sponse to stimuli. Excessive stimulation becomes irritating—as tickling does if it is continued for too long. Pleasure diminishes with overstimulation. Because it derives primarily from bodily awareness, it is subject to the body's limitations. Beautiful music becomes tiresome if one hears it to excess. Delicious food ceases to be enjoyable if one eats too much of it. Pleasure ceases to be pleasing, in time, *precisely because* it resonates with material conditions, which are in themselves inert. Pleasure is only a dim reflection of the bliss within.

Positive attitudes uplift the mind. Negative attitudes, on the other hand, take it slipping slowly downhill into a valley of private gloom. For as positive, happy attitudes make one receptive to bliss, negative attitudes estrange one from it.

Pleasure plays us false, for it tricks us into thinking we can receive happiness passively, instead of generating our own sense of well-being. Pleasure is basically something we *receive*. We absorb it into ourselves, like sponges, from already-existing waters. Ironically, people who live wholly for pleasure are *never* happy. Pleasure is self-indulgent, and inclines one therefore to be contractive. Happiness, on the other hand, is expansive to the consciousness, opening one to broader realities.

Pleasure can excite the mind. Music, for instance, can even exhilarate it. Because a person finds himself, in pleasure, reacting through his senses, however, his nerves become overstimulated. In time, his nerves reject that stimulation, and grow tired. Happiness, on the other hand, brings peace, not irritation, to the nervous system, for it raises one toward the source of bliss, within.

Pleasure can also be a release. Try pinching the flesh on your hand for a time, then release it. Notice how enjoyable the release feels. Release following any tension, or even pain, is in itself pleasurable. Desire, too, is a kind of "pinching." It can induce pain in the sense of a feeling of lack. Release is to a great extent, indeed, what people experience when they fulfill a desire.

What causes people to laugh after a good joke? As the story is told, the person relating it will often try to create a slight tension of anticipation in his listeners: uncertainty as to how the story will end. The "punch line" then brings a sudden, unexpected release. The laughter that ensues can be exhilarating. Both the release and that subsequent stimulation of laughter indicate some of the ways in which pleasure simulates happiness.

Such pleasure, too, is a counterfeit, for

whereas happiness invites higher states of awareness, laughter alone ties one to the senses. True happiness is calm. The exhilaration of laughter, however, makes one restless unless one deliberately redirects the energy it generates toward deeper understanding. Too often, otherwise, the excitement of laughter whips up restless waves in the mind. The energy it generates interferes with mental clarity.

The favorite scripture of Hindus, the *Bhagavad Gita,* states, "To the restless person, happiness is impossible."

I have found when lecturing that it helps occasionally to tell a funny story, so people will laugh, for in the emotional release of laughter they become more receptive. I consider it important, however, immediately after that to uplift people calmly toward clear understanding lest their laughter scatter, rather than focus, their attention.

An increase of energy, regardless of how it is produced, induces a heightened sense of well-being. In this sense even excitement can masquerade as happiness. If, however, one seeks happiness only in excitement, he ends up needing to rest his nerves. Excitement is exhausting, finally. The same is true for all human emotions— for example, the moods that accompany romantic love. The energy generated by excitement of any kind draws its power from mere expectations, not from the true source of energy in inner bliss.

Observe the shining eyes of a little child when he visits the zoo. Excitement gives him that energy. He is, indeed, overjoyed by it! It derives not from what he is seeing, but from the expectations he has formed of this outing. Excitedly he pulls his parents by the hand as he rushes along to see the monkeys, the zebras, the lions, the crocodiles. These exciting images exist only in his mind. The happiness he feels might be described as a visual echo. For echoes, as we all know, gradually die away: they don't renew themselves. And so it is that those images gradually fade in his mind.

Observe the child a few hours later. His enjoyment can no longer be reaffirmed. His senses having been overstimulated by so many impressions, his expectations have reached a surfeit. He now holds his parents back by the hand, pleading with them, "Mommy, Daddy, let's go home!" If they don't respond quickly enough, he begins to cry. What fun he has had! but the poor little fellow can stand only so much of it. Tired now, his energy is depleted and he no longer feels that former excitement.

Most people mistakenly equate happiness with excitement. If they plan a holiday, they will exclaim to their friends, "I'm so *excited* to be going!" Not many remark calmly, "I'm happy in going."

Their excitement is understandable, of course. People want to be *energetically* happy. If their energy creates too many ripples in the mind, however, instead of bringing it to a calm focus, their very capacity for enjoyment will be seriously hampered.

Suppose someone after merely glimpsing a beautiful view runs about shouting, "Look at that view, everybody! Just look at it! Those glorious shades of green! That grand sweep of the hills toward the sky! The majesty of the ocean beyond that valley!" Obviously, his mind will only be distracted. A person listening to beautiful music might keep time by waving his fingers about as if he were conducting an orchestra. In this outwardness, there can be no deep appreciation for the music. Fully to appreciate great music, one should be silently absorbed in listening.

Excitement stimulates the will. So also does happiness. How then do the two differ? In both cases, it is the will that generates energy. The exhilaration of excitement, however, takes the mind up, like a hooked fish, to the surface. The energy that happiness generates, on the other hand, takes one deeper into himself. Excitement overstimulates the nerves, but happiness calms them. Happiness, moreover, doesn't diminish with long exposure, whereas excitement ends eventually in fatigue; it brings boredom and disappointment in the end. To avoid such disappointment in life, try always to remain calm in yourself.

The masters mentioned in Chapter Two sought to guide people toward inner bliss. Think how a pirate, by contrast, would respond to such teaching. He'd ridicule it! His excitement on having all those glittering jewels run through his fingers, on beholding all that stolen gold glistening in the sunlight, would seem to him the very epitome of happiness. Detectives, when they try to solve a crime, are taught to ask, "*Cui Bono:* Who benefits?" The pirate would boast, "Well, *I* am the gainer!" He augments his wealth by his "trade" of robbing people. In the eyes of the law, too, he is the one who benefits. In the eyes of a higher law, however, the pirate is the loser. The consequences of his way of life bring him, not happiness, but misery.

People want happiness for the same reason they want pleasure: because, in their souls, they want bliss. Eventually, however, they learn that pleasure doesn't, in itself, produce happiness. Many people equate happiness with excitement, but doing so brings them, eventually, a deep sense of the purposelessness of their lives!

In *Die Fledermaus,* an operetta by Johann Strauss, Jr.,* a wealthy baron offers a reward to anyone who can succeed in making him laugh. Excessive wealth has reduced him to utter boredom; he despairs of ever being happy again. During a delightfully farcical sequence a young couple engage in ridiculous antics. At last the Baron bursts out, "Ha! Ha-ha! Ha-ha-ha!" Promptly then he announces, solemnly, "I laughed. You shall be rewarded."

Laughter generates excitement, which in turn generates energy. Laughter is not necessarily a sign of happiness, however. Only laughter that rises from the heart can *express* true happiness. Usually, what merriment expresses is only restlessness. People laugh without reason, to show they are excited. "How energetic I am!" they imply. "Doesn't that mean I am happy?" But they are *not* happy. They are merely jumping up and down mentally at their periphery. They think to inflate their happiness like a balloon, but in fact they deflate it—to the point of exhaustion.

---

*I attended a performance of this operetta with Paramhansa Yogananda in 1951 at the Hollywood Bowl, where a friend and student of his, Vladimir Rosing, was the visiting conductor. —*JDW*

Never delude yourself, then, in your quest for happiness by thinking you'll find it in constant giggling. (Isn't it usually over nothing?) If you want to be truly happy, learn to live at your own center. From that point alone can your happiness expand.

Study impartially the effects of pleasure, excitement, exhilaration, and release on people's happiness. These things are a masquerade of happiness. Like poison, they are irritants. Poison of course kills, but a tiny quantity of it can actually stimulate. The various expressions of pleasure, similarly, stimulate the will. The will, in turn, quickens the energy. The irritating effect of this stimulation, however, like poison, eventually drains one—as we saw in the case of that little child at the zoo.

Happiness goes on nourishing one's enthusiasm. The happy person is aglow with ever-fresh, *inner* energy. His nerves not frayed by excitement, he can cope effectively with every situation. He doesn't meet every crisis with a sudden adrenaline "rush," but with the calm address of one who is in command of himself.

Pleasure and the excitement that frequently accompanies it are only temporary, but their negative effects can be long-lasting. People who seek fulfillment only in pleasure find themselves at last prematurely old, tired, and disillusioned with life.

Pleasure, then, is indeed a counterfeit. Like counterfeit money, it may be circulated safely for a time, but after that it destroys one's happiness. Counterfeit money, as even governments discover if they overinflate their currency, destroys wealth. The counterfeit "money" of pleasure, similarly, if "circulated" too freely, destroys one's wealth of inner happiness. Excessive sensory indulgence depletes one's powers, to the point where one finds himself incapable of replenishing them, for his connection with the self within has been severed.

A simple rule for a long and happy life is this: Be always calmly happy, and happily calm; calmly active, and ever actively calm.

CHAPTER FIVE

Happiness Is Counterfeit Bliss

Happiness for most people begins with the thought, "This is how things ought to be!" Suffering comes with the opposite thought: "Things ought *not* to be as they are." Behind everything man does, his motivation never changes. It is to avoid suffering, and to find happiness.

Very easily, however, people fall into the habit of thinking they know already how things ought or ought not to be. They identify happiness with fixity instead of accepting life's natural flow. They become in time what I call "psychological antiques" — wanting nothing moved, nothing changed, nothing even improved. Stability is their concept of permanence. Permanence, however, is something the soul can have only in God.

Happiness is bliss outwardly directed toward the senses and their world of relativity and change. The desire that one's happiness be permanent is doomed to frustration despite the strong will that it endure. Bliss is eternal, but happiness is man's attempt to project bliss into a fleeting and alien environment. In that projection, he forms attachments to things temporal. Happiness, in its pretense of permanence, becomes simply another counterfeit, like pleasure.

People's search for outward stability is often visualized by them as a fixed place on earth, a home of their own. Imagine that place as they often conceive it: a picturesque cottage by the sea, its entrance graced by a rose trellis, its well-manicured lawn bordered by colorful flowers, the garden enlivened by gay song birds. The interior of the cottage is cozily furnished with good books, good paintings, good furniture. "Wee Nook" we'll call it: Countless "dream cottages" bear that quaint, if somewhat cloying, name! This is a place for putting down one's roots.

Gaze mentally at the flowers. Stroll peacefully through that well-tended garden. Listen appreciatively to the birds' songs. Sit comfortably in a living room armchair, and read a good book. Chat in the evening with good friends. Doesn't all this suggest happiness unalloyed?

Now, visualize the dream lasting . . . and lasting . . . and *lasting!* No matter how pleasant, might it not last *too long?* Ten years might already be overdoing it—but *eternity?* Any happiness you find at "Wee Nook" would certainly become stale, eventually; your "fulfillment" might well become more a burden to you than a joy. Someday you'd surely find yourself crying out in desperation, "Somebody—something: Please knock me on the head to convince me I'm still alive!" Boredom is a very different condition, certainly, from bliss!

Everyone wants to avoid suffering: so far, so good. Everyone wants to find happiness. So far—well, exactly *how* good?

What everyone *really* wants is bliss. Happiness defined as a sort of misty contentment is by no means the bliss our souls want. Like basement-printed money, it is a counterfeit; too much of it diffuses one's very concept of bliss. To a mind full of attachments, bliss seems almost a threat. A cottage by the sea is something the ego, at least, can handle without effort. But *bliss?* Bliss requires total absorption. Few people are ready to be *all that* happy! They *need* suffering, to spur them toward ever-higher aspiration.

A bird, after twenty years of living in a cage, would be afraid to leave it. Were the cage door opened, the bird would cower at the back, dreading the flight that is, for all that, perfectly natural for it.

Man, at the thought of absorption in bliss,

faces two major challenges. First, to his mind, bliss implies a need for exerting high energy. Second, the concept of *absolute* consciousness seems to him overwhelming.

A mother once scolded her infant child, "Come on now, Johnny, you're a big boy now. Don't be such a baby!"

The toddler, alarmed at this reminder that he ought to be growing up, replied, "But I *like* being a baby!" Many adults are like little Johnny: They, too, would rather remain as they are. They *like* being ordinary, unpretentious, down-to-earth, humble, and any other self-definition they require for reining in their imagination! They *like* being, as the expression is, "average Joes." They *like* participating in the herd instinct. (Evidently they'd rather drown *with* others than alone! For they conveniently overlook that the "average Joe" is probably far from happy.) Absolute bliss strikes them as horrifying; they identify almost fiercely with their ego-self, and whip up clouds of distraction to protect it from any challenge. Perhaps they hope to find safety in ignorance. (Isn't this a common saying: "Ignorance is bliss"?) Perhaps they know they'll have to face bliss eventually. If so however, their preference, for now, is to "sit this one out."

Absoluteness may be philosophically sound,

but were a person faced with the prospect of attaining it *today, this very moment,* he might well hesitate like that bird, muttering fearfully, "Not yet, dear God! Give me time to enjoy my present state just a little while longer!" It was the great Saint Augustine himself who in his youth pleaded, "Lord, make me good, *but not yet!*"

When a person is informed that salvation includes infinite consciousness, he may ask, "What sort of 'divine promise' is *that?* Isn't it meant to be *comforting?*" Small wonder the orthodox religions everywhere offer "prettified" versions of that promise. Jesus Christ's ringing commandment, "Be ye therefore perfect, even as your Father which is in heaven is perfect," is overlooked. Stirring words like these in the scriptures tend to be played back for the public at a reduced volume—indeed, they tend to be ignored altogether. "Kinder" versions are offered instead: for instance, "Be ye therefore good, as your heavenly Father is good."

The Moslem heaven is described so as to be attractive to the senses. Heaven for the Hindu is described in allegorical images, which people often accept as factual, of souls dancing through eternity with Lord Krishna in the graceful "*rasa lila.*" Suggested to Christians is an eternity of harp playing and singing with choirs of angels.

A common obstacle on the spiritual path

was described by the ancient *rishi* (sage) Patan-jali. He called it, *"false notions."* One such false notion is that the attainment of high states of consciousness must require extraordinary strain. The "happy" clam in the last chapter, were it asked to proceed consciously to higher stages of awareness, might protest, "But I *like* being a 'happy clam'! So what if I merely open and close my shell, and ingest tiny organisms? So what if I'm not even really happy at all, and find no particular pleasure in anything? I'm set-tled. I'm comfortable. I'm just a clam. *Don't ask me to be anything more!"*

Yet animals higher up in the evolutionary scale would not relinquish their pleasures vol-untarily, simple as those pleasures are, for a clam's existence. The gazelle leaping through the tall grass of an African veldt would not will-ingly curtail its exuberance to wallow in mud with the turtles. The nightingale wouldn't give up its beautiful singing to croak by a pond with the frogs. And man wouldn't want to return to the comparatively twilight consciousness of the lower animals. If, moreover, he has attained a certain degree of refinement, he would be un-willing to return to living like others who limit their pleasures to the table, the barroom, and the bedroom. Creatures at every stage of evolution cling to what is familiar to them.

Familiarity gives them their sense of security. And so, they may meet the call to higher awareness with stout resistance.

Nothing of import is ever *lost,* however, in the long climb of evolution toward Conscious Bliss. Reluctance to move higher than one's present state must be dismissed as simply another "false notion." People by their reluctance merely betray ignorance as to where their true interests lie.

The principal challenge bliss presents is the demand that one's ego be abandoned. Human beings define themselves in terms of their bodies. They think of themselves as having a specific age, name, nationality, sex, and social position. These do not, however, truly define us at all.

It was the divine consciousness that brought all beings and all things into manifestation. To *manifest* something is not the same as to *create* it. God did not *mold* us from the outside, like works of sculpture. He *became* us, as we ourselves "become" our dreams, which seem to have an existence of their own, but are really just the form taken on by a part of our consciousness. When that consciousness is withdrawn, they simply cease to exist. A physical analogy would be the way a seed grows to become a tree, starting from the center, then growing outward. Before God manifested the universe, only He existed: timeless, spaceless, Conscious Bliss. He is the essence of everything in existence. *We ourselves* are pure consciousness. *We ourselves* are pure bliss.

One might think people would offer no resistance to this truth, once they felt reassured that no strain was involved in its attainment, and once they realized that this state is accompanied by absolute peace and perfect joy.

The hair stands on end, however, at the "news" that the ego must be abandoned! Everyone sees himself as simply Doug Johnson or Mary Jones. Must this long-familiar identity really be sacrificed? The simple answer is, *Yes!* Indeed, the thought that this surrender is a sacrifice is only a "false notion." In infinite consciousness, not even self-awareness, ultimately, is lost: it is simply transformed. This is a law of life, as well as of physics: Nothing, in essence, can be either created or destroyed. Doug Johnson and Mary Jones will never abandon their essential individuality. That self, when it is merged in God, can be resurrected at any time by people's prayers, or by the will of God.

Man's dread at the thought of being omnipresent may be compared to the dread of the caged bird. In perfect freedom, one discovers who he really is. Like that little bird soaring upward in flight—the life for which it was always intended—the soul expands with an infinite sense of rest in Conscious Bliss.

Freedom should not terrify anyone. Of the many in every age, culture, and religion who have attained it, *not one* has ever expressed rue at the accomplishment. Nor has any of them gloomily accused the scriptures of being "pied pipers" leading the unwary to their destruction. Everyone, rather, after attaining release in Conscious Bliss, feels himself blessed to embrace even martyrdom, if by so doing he can share his discovery with others.

For it must be added, of course, that so noble an ideal could not be offered to people without exposing oneself to persecution. Human ignorance will not stand by silently and make no protest! Persecution of one sort or another has been the lot of every saint and prophet who ever lived.

In Mark Twain's novel, *The Adventures of Huckleberry Finn,* two tricksters fool half the people in a town into paying good money for a fraudulent show. After an absurdly brief spectacle, the citizens, realizing they've been bilked, decide among themselves to praise the evening's "entertainment" lavishly to everyone else in town, that the rest of them may be persuaded to attend the second evening's performance. Thus, the whole town gets involved in the fiasco, and no one remains in a strategic position of being able to ridicule anyone else. The entire town turns out for the third evening, intent on revenge. On this evening however, the miscreants, after collecting everyone's money, make good their escape, taking with them their ill-gotten gains from all three of the performances.

Skeptics suspect similar shenanigans when they are urged to love God. Howls of laughter greet the jokes they tell about preachers who hoodwink their congregations. What a pity! The boon all human beings seek from life is one that only religion can bestow. There is, however, this difference between formal religion and individual spirituality: Spirituality inspires no need to *convince* anybody. One who follows the inward path feels only a desire to love God ever more deeply. He gives spiritual love freely to anyone who will accept it. Mockery would besmirch such honest devotion. But once bliss has been attained, it seems a privilege to give all that one has and is for the upliftment of others. To serve God everywhere and in everyone is one's greatest joy.

To transcend ego-consciousness is the supreme test for every aspirant. Though all men are destined to embrace it eventually, and all will do so joyfully, the ego puts up a fierce struggle before it willingly surrenders its fiefdom. It is natural that it should do so, for it is only acting in self-protection. The instinct of self-preservation is deeply ingrained in all; born in ego-consciousness, they naturally define themselves as their egos. Thus, the ego cannot be simply reasoned away: It must be overcome a step at a time by deep meditation. The bird, observing its cage door still open, may attempt a brief sortie—then withdraw again hastily with palpitating heart. It may require several more attempts before it will spread its wings and take to the air. What a delight, then, to find that freedom is its *normal* state! The consciousness of self, too, must be released *voluntarily* into the Infinite. For our eternal birthright, along with bliss, is free will.

It is easy enough to see why man, once he has achieved a measure of happiness, decides to remain satisfied with what he has. Why, he thinks, strive for anything more? The divine plan, however, is for nothing outside himself to satisfy him for long. Human happiness was never meant to be permanent. It is a *reminder,* only, of the inner bliss of the soul. Though there must be a *will* to be happy, human nature contains much that is beyond human control. Indeed, the will, unaided, is faltering at best, and susceptible to feelings that rise both unbidden and unexpected from currents deep in the subconscious, which run darkly "through caverns measureless to man."* Despite every affirmation to the contrary, human happiness is unreliable.

In the last chapter, I minimized these subconscious influences in order to make an essential point: that happiness must be *willed*. It is also true, however, that the storms through which all must pass before their ships reach a safe harbor in God are numerous and, at times, violent. The storms do not, of course, negate the need for good seamanship. Human smugness, meanwhile, can be defeated only by suffering. Suffering is man's constant spur toward wisdom.

God says to the soul, "My child, I have divine ambrosia to give you, but if you prefer drinking water from the unclean fountain of sense pleasures, I will not insist. I have prepared a royal banquet for you, but if you'd rather play with mud pies, remain enjoying them for now. When you are hungry, come to Me: The banquet will be waiting for you."

The compromise that is human happiness, however, is unbecoming to the kingly dignity of

*The quote is from Coleridge's poem, "Kubla Khan."

the soul. Human beings are rays of God's infinite light. How long—indeed, how many lifetimes!—has it taken every human being to attain his present level of understanding! And how arduous has been the climb! It is in everyone's own interest to embrace a higher destiny. God asks man only, "Is it really unclean water and mud pies that you prefer?"

Many influences arise in the subconscious and in the surrounding world. Not a few of those influences are negative. Release can come not by focusing on them, for to do so only increases their power. Release comes, rather, by deepening one's determination to live in conscious bliss. The will to be happy is opposed constantly, and is weakened by the fact that it can so easily be misdirected. The will to bliss, however, is reinforced by Conscious Bliss itself. That Conscious Bliss actually provides the strength for overcoming all delusions. Obscuring clouds of negativity can be dispersed only by bliss-winds. If, then (to use another metaphor), a room is in darkness, the darkness cannot be driven out by beating at it with a stick: One must turn on the light!

There is a story in the *Mahabharata,* one of India's great epics, in which Dronacharya, supreme preceptor in the martial arts, asks Arjuna to shoot the head off a bird that has been tied to the top of a tall tree. Arjuna's cousins and brothers, who are students under the same teacher, have already been asked by him to perform this feat. None has succeeded. "What do you see?" Dronacharya asked each of them in turn. "I see you, Master," was their reply. "I see that tall tree. I see the bird." Their responses varied, of course, but what they all thought he wanted was a demonstration of their powers of observation.

"What do *you* see, Arjuna?" Drona asked.

"I see the head of the bird," came the reply.

"Nothing else?"

"Nothing. Only the head of the bird."

"Go ahead: Shoot!" cried Dronacharya. He knew that this, his prize pupil, would hit the mark. And so he did.

In every undertaking, the way to "hit the mark" is to ignore every distraction and center all one's attention on the object of success. A strong will can drive away even clouds that obscure the earth's sun. Not for the spiritual hero, the hand-wringing lament, "Oh, *but think* of the difficulties I face!"

The Buddha, after years of spiritual seeking, seated himself firmly one day on the ground beneath a Bodhi tree and made his famous vow: "Let this body disintegrate, but until I have solved life's mystery *I never more will move* from this spot!"

Satan himself — *Mara* (Death) as he was known then — appeared before him to break his heroic resolve. Beautiful maidens appeared and danced temptingly before him. Untold wealth and power were offered him. Throughout this dazzling display Buddha sat, unmoved.

At last, with flinchless will, he rapped his knuckles firmly on the ground and spoke these immortal words: "*Mara,* I have conquered thee!" The vision fled. In that moment, his soul broke its mortal bonds and soared outward in skies of infinity.

The bliss Buddha attained is the desire of the ages. Great was his sacrifice; for most people that sacrifice would have been impossible. Yet it was actually no sacrifice at all! It might be described better as an investment. For what is it, to relinquish something so small as the ego for such vast returns? As long as man is trapped in his ego, he sees the goal of bliss as remote, and settles instead for immediate, though tinsel, "victories." These always prove false, however, in the end. Behind every rosebush of pleasure lies the cobra of misery, coiled, ready to strike. And beyond the wall that surrounds the little garden of human happiness stretches a vast desert, relentlessly ready to encroach.

A young woman, "happy" in her recent marriage to a man of questionable character, wanted felicitations from her older sister. That sister, a true friend, replied earnestly, "Indeed, I do wish you happiness. I only hope you'll be as happy in five years as you are today."

"Oh, five years!" exclaimed the younger one dismissively. "Who cares what happens in *five years!*"

The problem is, whatever happens at any future time will be very much *today,* when that time arrives. We should live our present day so conscientiously that our future will not be, five years or five lifetimes from now, *distressingly* "today." For the fact is, the same ego will have to accept whatever fruits have grown on its tree of life. Does the farmer abstain from planting seeds with the lame excuse that the time for harvest is in the future?

A justification people frequently offer for why they accept a compromise happiness is, "Everybody else does what I'm doing, and *they* seem happy enough. Why should I be any different?" That premise requires close examination. *Is* "everybody" really so happy? If one could be an invisible presence in their homes, he would behold a scene very different from the one they display to the world. In sober truth, *no one is really happy.* The happiness people think they've found is only a sign that life's starker realities are, for now, being successfully held at arms' length by distractions. No major catastrophe looms: Therefore—they tell themselves—they are "happy," or at any rate sufficiently so not to want jarring questions put to them!

A woman once came to the Buddha and pleaded with him to restore life to her little son, who had died that morning. Buddha replied by asking her to bring him a small quantity of mustard oil with which he might anoint the body. "Take care, however," he cautioned, "that the oil come from a home that has not seen death."

The woman left him, full of confidence. A week later she returned in despair. Not a single home had met that condition. Buddha's aim had been to teach her a truth he himself had discovered years earlier: Death stalks in the footsteps of every human being. Death might be described, indeed, as the only enduring reality of life.

The "happy ending" of many a Hollywood movie is a myth. The closing scene fades with everybody smiling victoriously, or tenderly, or gratefully as the case may be. Fairy tales end typically with the words, "And they lived happily ever after." Thus are disposed of (with indecent haste, one might almost add!) subsequent years of compromise, bickering, and bitterness!

Bliss beckons to us from behind every human satisfaction and disappointment. To attain it may be difficult, but considering the plain truth that *there really is no alternative,* one might call it the only purchase in the marketplace that is worth the price!

Happiness must be willed. It cannot, however, be *manufactured.* Certainly, the possibility exists for human beings to be happy. Their happiness, however, cannot be anything but fleeting and imperfect. To the extent that it is experienced, bliss filters down from the higher self into their human awareness.

Buddha's exercise of such extraordinary will power raises an important question: How much of the spiritual path demands an exertion of man's own will, and how much is possible only by the grace of God? From Buddha's example, the conclusion might be drawn that victory depends entirely on man's own efforts. This conclusion would be mistaken.

One of the age-old debates in religion revolves around this question. Some of the ancient teachings — Buddhism, notably — emphasize self-effort almost to the exclusion of everything else. Others—Islam, as an example— stress the need for complete surrender to God's will. Both teachings are right; they are simply two sides of one coin, each one meant simply as a corrective to common misconceptions. Each teaching taken by itself, however, is a "false notion." Passivity, for its part, can deaden the will. Self-effort, again, can lead one astray if it is based on ego-affirmation.

People sometimes justify passivity with the excuse, "God is the Doer; we must not stand in His way." One who makes this statement errs by underestimating his innate power to do good. To leave everything to God's will can seem to absolve one of any need to rely on his own conscience. It can even become an excuse, therefore, for committing evil.

Those on the other hand who tell themselves, "My salvation is my own responsibility entirely" err by separating their own power from grace (which is to say, from the power of God). The goal of conscious evolution is, eventually, to unite. Separation is necessary only for a time, to focus one's efforts. (Hence the need, for a time, for the human ego.) The Infinite Power provides us with food to eat and the energy with which to digest it. Man's is the responsibility, however, for putting the food into his mouth, chewing, then swallowing it. It is also man's responsibility to choose wisely what he eats. He must *cooperate* with the law and with divine grace. He cannot ask God to do *everything* for him. The Lord demands *reciprocity*.

To achieve a right balance on the path to Conscious Bliss, the will of the individual must be directed toward union with Conscious Bliss, in loving self-offering. It was only after years of spiritual practices that Buddha could utter his Great Vow. Before that, his will was not yet sufficiently well tuned to Conscious Bliss itself.

Grace may be compared to the sunlight on the side of a building. The people within must part their own curtains to *receive* the light. Self-effort is needed for parting them. Mankind cannot, however, create the sunlight.

To part a curtain is, of course, relatively easy, whereas it takes enormous will power, as well as deep devotion, to open the heart's shutters to God's love. Salvation is possible only because sincerity and courage *attract* the strength needed for its attainment. Conscious Bliss, to which all mankind aspires whether knowingly or not, *gives the sincere seeker its own power of victory.*

Not only was Buddha's resolution heroic: It was *inspired.* Had it not been, his vow would surely have failed. Inspiration is the key to everything. It will be the subject of the next chapter. For now, it should be pointed out that inspiration, like happiness, must be *received;* it cannot be manufactured. Because all power resides in Conscious Bliss itself, there is hope for humanity. Spiritual success can be attained by everyone. Therefore it was that the Christian Bible proclaimed, "As many as *received* him, to them *gave he power* to become the sons of God."

Know, meanwhile, that although your path will lead you as far afield as *you* yourself desire, it must turn back eventually — *inevitably* — in as large a loop as *you* choose to make it, to its starting point in *your own self.*

CHAPTER SIX

The Source of Inspiration

Man cuts himself off from the great river of life, then laments that his life is dry. He separates his ego from the vast ocean of consciousness, then complains that he feels alienated. If his work is creative (for instance, as an artist), he may try to produce inspiration from the barren soil of his own brain — and wonder, then, why his work lacks vitality. Can the crops grow, when there is no rain?

Even intellectual brilliance is mind-born. However intelligent the brain, it cannot actually *produce* inspiration. The best it can do is *invite* insight from a higher level of wisdom. Inspiration can only be *received*. Receptivity, then, is the key to true genius. If a person wants to be inspired, he must *draw* on the well of inspiration. And when inspiration comes, he must rigidly exclude the ego-instigated thought, "This is *my* inspiration."

For if inspiration is true, it is impersonal. It comes to him who can set aside his likes and dislikes and ask himself, "What is right? What is true? What is appropriate in this particular situation?"

One must lose his ego, in a sense, in the flow of inspiration. At the same time, he must use discrimination, for his role in the creative process is to *filter* whatever inspirations he receives. Thus, although inspiration is impersonal, it must also be individualized. Creativity, in other words, is a cooperative act. The insights one receives must be filtered through one's own experience and understanding.

Man never acts by his power alone. He couldn't even breathe were not air, and the very power of breathing, provided to him by Nature. Living is a cooperative act also. Man errs only if he intrudes his sense of personal importance into his contribution to the general good. Otherwise, everyone is able to contribute something, and his contribution may, to the extent especially that he can filter higher inspiration, be a great help to many.

Unfortunately, people commonly do intrude their egos, even when their involvement is minimal. Thereby, they muddy the crystalline flow of inspiration. A paint maker may boast, "I'm responsible for the beautiful paintings artists execute." Simply then he explains, "I made their paints." His claim would be outrageous were it not so commonly paraphrased. Most people, possibly, are guilty of a similar outrage, for man sees himself as the centerpiece in his personal universe. Thus, the farmer may claim his share of the credit, since it was he who grew the plants from which the canvas was made. The weaver may claim his share also, since he wove the canvas. The carpenter says, "I made the frame." The brush maker boasts, "I made the brush the artist used." And the paint maker? We've already seen how he preens himself on *his* contribution! The artist, finally, is of all people the most likely to say, "Look at *my* new landscape!"

Meanwhile, who was it created the scene from which the landscape was painted? Who made the material for the cloth? the wood for the frame? the hairs for the brush? the pigments for the paint? We need to deepen our awareness of the part played by God in our lives. Even the belief—quite justified, I might add—that each of us has a role to play in life was planted in our minds by the Lord Himself.

The truths we've discussed so far are important to an understanding of true faith. For faith is no mere *expectation*. Nor is it wishful thinking imposed by man on objective reality. It is more also than belief, which is simply hypothesis. Faith is born of direct experience. Ultimately, it is the clear recognition that God alone *exists;* that only He has the power to free us forever from all suffering, and to grant eternal bliss.

Religious people, aware of their need for God, may try to satisfy it, if they are Hindus, by chanting *Ramnam;* or, if they are Christians, by singing hymns and participating in the Eucharist. If they are Moslems, they will perform *namaj* (bowing toward Mecca). Certain religious groups worship spiritual images; others repudiate images altogether. In every case, what all of them seek is one thing only: upliftment. Spiritual upliftment is not in itself either Hindu, Christian, Moslem, Buddhist, or Jewish. It might, in mundane experience, be compared to the feeling people have after eating a good meal. The contentment an Indian feels after a good curry dinner is no different from that of an American after a Thanksgiving banquet. The upliftment people experience, similarly, from attending an inspiring religious service is essentially the same whether it be in temple, church, vihara, mosque, or synagogue. As satisfaction after a good meal is simply satisfaction, and not "curry satisfaction" or "Thanksgiving satisfaction," so inspiration is, simply, inspiration.

Inspiration derived from worship depends not only on uplifted expectations, but on people's *receptivity*. It must be *invited*. If it comes, it must then be *received*.

Were one to try swimming in an empty pool, he might buoy himself up briefly with the affirmation that there is an abundance of water in the pool. A mere moment later, however, he would find his affirmation alone to be absurdly inadequate.

God's response to prayer is not merely a delusion, born of self-persuasion. One need only put prayer to the test to find to what extent it works, and to what extent it is ineffective. The results of prayer depend entirely on its *quality* of thought and feeling. God never disappoints sincere aspiration, though He may not always respond as people expect Him to.

Inspiration has a reality of its own. The upliftment it brings, too, is its own reality. It may vary in appearance like the colored lights of a Christmas tree, but in essence it is simply light. The electricity flowing into those lights is uniform. It is only in color that the lights differ. Conscious Bliss, the very source of existence, is always the same whether it be called God, Allah, Jehovah, or Brahman. The differences in the religions of the world are only "colorations" given by the mind of man. Whatever differences exist in the flow of grace and power depend on the individual's sincerity, and not on the outer forms his worship takes.

Prayer and worship, when sincerely offered, attract definite blessings. The Christian's spiritual experiences are no different *in essence* from the Hindu's, the Buddhist's, the Moslem's, or those of any serious spiritual aspirant. The experiences are simply appropriate to the demands of the heart. A Hindu may behold visions of Krishna or Kali. A Christian may see Jesus Christ or the Virgin Mary. A Buddhist may see Buddha. If the vision is true, as many indeed are, it exalts the beholder. A true vision brings about deep changes in the beholder, and sometimes also in the objective world around him. Divine experiences transcend all sectarian differences. They are not personal, but are granted to those who have no selfish motives or ego-attachment.

God responds to love, not to "correct" definitions. He never "plays favorites." In Conscious Bliss, all divine expressions are manifestations of the same, infinite Spirit, just as countless waves are manifestations of the same sea.

Inspiration may also be a specific response to sincere demands made of it. To a mathematician it will come in mathematical, not in musical, terms. To a poet it will come as poetic, not as scientific, insights. The upliftment which accompanies true inspiration is its one constant feature. The nostalgic longing for God felt by a Christian singing the Gregorian chants, and the sweetness felt by a Hindu chanting the *Mahamantra,* both produce an upliftment of consciousness. God, as I said, watches the heart. He responds lovingly to expressions of love in whatever religion they are offered.

Too much attention to form, however, can create a disturbance in a person's devotion, diverting it from the expression of spontaneous love. Were a human lover to explain too precisely the nature of his feelings for his beloved, she might well doubt his sincerity. The deciding factor, when worshiping God, is one's openness to divine love. The shrine at which people worship matters for the devotion expressed there. The shrine itself is only the husk: Love is the seed. The important thing is that the seed contain *life.*

The affection a little girl expresses for her doll is not reciprocated, yet it helps her to deepen her *capacity* for love. A mother playing with her baby may not receive in return the response she'd like, but in her playing she deepens the quality of motherly love. Both mother and baby, consequently, grow more sensitive to the nuances of love. The vital thing, similarly, in our relationship with God is that we deepen our love for Him. Even if at first He seems unresponsive, devotion itself is ennobling.

God *never* ignores any sincere expression of love. If we persist in trying to win His response, the Lord Himself will pour out blessings in abundance. Were He never to nourish our hearts with the very sweetness of devotion, our devotion itself would grow dry, like a river after seasons of no rain. Even the power of loving derives from Him; it cannot be generated solely by man. Pray also, therefore, for the grace to love Him ever more deeply.

Religion without love is superstition. Attempts at conversion may in fact only hinder spiritual development, unless the attempt inspires fresh aspiration in the heart.

A missionary many years ago in Ranchi, India, succeeded in converting a village of "aborigines" to Christianity.* Several months later he returned to see how they were prospering in their new faith. He was appalled to find them seated on the ground, chanting *Ramnam* (the names of Rama).

---

*"Aborigines" is the term Western scholars often apply, quaintly, to certain backward groups in India. Their claim, which is made with perhaps a measure of nationalistic smugness, is that India's ancient civilization was of foreign and relatively recent origin. Nothing in Indian tradition itself, however, endorses that view.

"What are you doing?!" He cried in outrage.

"Why, what do you mean?" they inquired, perplexed. "This is our religion."

The villagers, in their simplicity, had understood that what really matters in religion is *pure intention*. Love, not correct dogma, is what attracts God. Those villagers loved Jesus for the purity of his love for God. They loved Rama also, for the same reason. Why could not the Infinite Lord be adored differently in different contexts? Their simple faith inspired them to see Rama and Jesus as expressions of divine love. Were not both those saviors equally deserving of devotion?

Representatives of formal religion may object, "But only Jesus Christ (or Rama, or Krishna, or Buddha) can grant actual salvation." This question, however, is not man's to decide. Surely it is presumptuous to declare, "I accept [fill in the blank] as *my* savior!" Man's duty is to love God. God's part alone is it to decide whether a person really merits salvation. The divine decision is always based on the simple issue of purity. Therefore it was that Jesus Christ said, "Blessed are the pure in heart, for they shall see God."

Water flows by many channels to the sea. Neither its goal nor its downward direction ever changes. What does it matter how the sea is named? The word for "sea" in French is *la mer.* In Italian, it is *il mare.* Hindi speakers call it *sagara.* There may be certain primitive hill tribes who don't even know that the sea exists. What difference does it make? Rivers flow downward just the same, and all of them flow toward the sea. The vastness that is their goal is in any case beyond ordinary human comprehension.

The same may be said of God. There is little point in trying to define Him "correctly." The important thing is that our love flow toward Him, and not away into tiny, separate channels which evaporate in the harsh light of disappointment. It is a waste of effort to try with the intellect to comprehend the vastness of God.

The goal of all desire is Conscious Bliss. Without that goal clearly in mind, religion can easily become idol worship. For idolatry doesn't mean the worship of graven images. It means paying homage to things that are unconscious, and incapable themselves of expanding one's consciousness. Regardless of the formal tenets to which one subscribes, if, while praying to God, he harbors a consuming desire for money, his real object of worship is money. Money is his idol, the "graven image" enshrined on the altar of his heart. Most people, in fact, worship mammon. Most people, therefore, are idolaters. In their pantheon, God holds a very subordinate position. Indeed, most religionists, whatever their religious beliefs, don't really worship God at all, or Christ, Krishna, Kali, or Brahman. What they worship is — simply — their own ignorance!

Sensory awareness encourages the pursuit of pleasure. Awareness, on the other hand, of life's universal goal, which is the avoidance of suffering and the attainment of happiness, inspires one to seek bliss. No complex theology is needed to justify this goal. It is self-evidently what all men deeply desire, whether their hope of attainment be pinned on Buddha, Jesus Christ, Krishna, Mohammed, or any teacher or teaching. Gold may be cast into innumerable shapes, but *as gold* its value remains constant. The "gold" of Conscious Bliss, similarly, never changes, regardless of how many ways it is cast by the human mind.

Everyone is then, in this sense, religious, even if he lacks religious conviction altogether. In the future, as people grow to understand this truth, the sectarian barriers that for centuries have divided mankind will fall. To worship God as Conscious Bliss will bring to everyone the awareness of the deep kinship that unites all life. Whether at present people recognize this truth or not, it is what all of them seek, saints and sinners alike. Their goal is the attainment of union with God—with ever-existing, ever-conscious, ever-new Bliss, or *Satchidananda*.

People who doubt the existence of God need only develop realistic expectations of life, and of themselves. Error is but ignorance, with its consequently misplaced expectations. The sensualist, excited by his physical passion, mistakes that agitation for happiness, and ignores the many warning signals within himself and, outwardly, from others. Much later, only, does he discover that his expectations were founded on a colossal delusion. Sin is error not because it displeases God, but because it causes disillusionment, and deep suffering, in the sinner himself. God, however, is above all pleasure and displeasure. He resides eternally in absolute, Conscious Bliss.

Hell, so greatly feared by so many, can be experienced right here on earth. Its suffering can be intensified after death, to be sure, for the physical body with its thick walls of flesh is no longer there to offer some protection. The feelings, after they cease to be held in check by the rational faculty, are unleashed, and may be correspondingly intense. Everlasting hell, however, is a fallacy. Eternity cannot be defined in temporal terms. Even a billion years, in eternity, would not rate the blinking of an eyelid!*

It is the nature of suffering for the sufferer to imagine he'll never again emerge from his darkness. Every avenue of escape seems forever closed to him. No alternate realities seem even imaginable. When, subsequently, his consciousness expands with compassion and understanding, he discovers that it was he himself who closed those avenues—in his own mind! Despair made him abandon hope and, with it, all aspiration. Though he felt rejected, it was he himself who did the "rejecting."

A certain student of mine was consumed by self-doubt. Fearfully he asked me one day, "Will I ever fall from the spiritual path?"

"How could you?" I replied. "Everyone in the world is on the spiritual path!"†

And so it is. And so must it ever be.

---

*Imagine a person condemned to hell for eternity over some act he committed in a state of spiritual immaturity. Imagine, then, a fellow "inmate" asking him after, say, a couple of billion years, "What are *you* down here for?" Might he not reply, "Well, I can't really recall. It all seems to have happened so very long ago!" To imagine a temporary cause producing so permanent an effect seems worse than unreasonable: It is barbaric!

†He did, however, several years later abandon the spiritual practices I had taught him.

CHAPTER SEVEN

Religion and Spirituality

"Everyone in the world is on the spiritual path." So ended the last chapter. By no means everyone, however, is aware of being on a path at all. Most people see their efforts to avoid sorrow and find happiness as episodic, not as the unchanging motivation behind everything they do.

Spirituality is often, but not often accurately, identified with religiosity. Although one naturally expects the two to be synonymous, they differ in several important ways. Spirituality is conscious aspiration, and is therefore individual. Formal religion, on the other hand, is a branch of civilized society—like business, politics, and the arts. It may be described as a social activity, designed to uplift humanity generally, and institutionalized to benefit as many people as possible. Spirituality, by contrast, is relatively exclusive, for it demands not only personal involvement but serious personal effort. Its ideals challenge the integrity of all who aspire to the truth.

Religion asks, instead, conformity to what might be called a "law of averages": lowering the heights to which people are expected to aspire, and—by acceptance of the desire for temporal fulfillment as right and natural—filling in the depths from which they are expected to climb. Formal religion, essentially, is outward, public, and (to gain the widest acceptance) a dilution of the highest truth. Spirituality's focus, on the other hand, is inward, personal, and (for the greatest personal gain) uncompromising. Religion is intended to be embraced by all; its teachings, therefore, are relatively easy to follow. By contrast, the demands of the spiritual path may seem austere, but their austerity is only a seeming. For life's true goal, which is to avoid sorrow and attain bliss, while wonderfully inspiring is also exacting. People's eyes reveal the contrast persuasively. Inner joy shines brightly in the eyes of those who live by high spiritual ideals. In the eyes of those who accept the compromises religion offers them, there are still lingering shadows of pain.

Spirituality requires one to assume personal responsibility for his own development. Formal religion makes fewer such requirements. It is, in a sense, a social contract between man and God, drawn up by religious institutions. The main responsibility of the individual in religious matters is that he accept the rituals and dogmas his institution has prescribed for him. Assumed on his behalf is the burden of determining the difference between truth and error, right and wrong, more or less as one leaves to lawyers the burden of clarifying legal matters. Religious tradition, then, like legal precedents, serves the purpose of perpetuating the practices that have been established.

There is a natural opposition between formal religion and the sciences. The pioneering efforts of science, which have uncovered countless numbers of Nature's secrets, provide a very different view of reality from religion's. Science rejects altogether the idea of a contract between man and his maker. It seeks to *discover* the facts of things, whereas religion simply *declares* truth, claiming that it was revealed to mankind long ago and never changes. Science's ongoing search for the facts poses a clear threat, therefore, to the concept of revelation. Religion, under pressure of countless and incontrovertible new facts, has had to accept its need to co-exist with science, and has therefore admitted that there do seem to be higher and lower levels of reality. Religion cannot change its insistence, however, that the higher level will, in the end, prove the only true one.

The path of spirituality stands in contrast to both religion and science. In some ways, however, it is more like science, for it, also, *seeks* truth rather than simply declaring it. The spiritual teachings do announce the discoveries that have been made by individual seekers (comparable to scientific researchers), but, like material science, they urge people to verify every claim, and not to remain satisfied with mere belief or mere assertion no matter how convincingly it is stated. Like science, moreover, which contemplates no fixed conclusion to its seeking, spiritual development is never ending. The only "end" it contemplates is endlessness! There is, however, one essential difference between the discoveries of the spiritual search and those of science: Whereas the spiritual search, like that of science, is continuous, its discoveries once made are universal and unvarying. The spiritual path, then, achieves something science will never achieve, for the phenomena explored by science are themselves subject to numerous shifts in perspective. Reason, too — the tool science uses — keeps the mind penned within the narrow enclosure of sensory perception. It cannot perceive with the far greater clarity of true intuition. Science, moreover, though it reasons from facts and doesn't draw conclusions from untested theories as theology does, is only slightly less shackled than theology is. It clings to its laws, sometimes even fiercely, as theology clings to its dogmas. The spiritual teachings, by contrast, urge people not to be satisfied with definitions, but to soar upward in direct perception until eternal truth is *experienced,* as it were, "face to face."

The world's religions, from a study of their dogmas, seem in wide disagreement with one another. Science itself, though generally assenting to facts that have been proved, is by no means open to "inconvenient" ones even after they've been proved to the satisfaction of a young generation of scientists. Scientists too can be dogmatic, in other words, when their view of reality has been boxed by lifelong habit. They are human beings, after all. Even so, science—unlike religion—has been known to change some of its "fixed" dogmas officially from time to time, when the proofs have become incontrovertible.

The spiritual teachings, by contrast, have never had to be changed, for although they are not stated dogmatically, people of deep spiritual insight in every country, every age, and every religion have declared the same experiences of truth. Regardless of cultural and religious heritage — some of those seers were actually illiterate, and therefore unfamiliar with their own heritage—they have announced the same basic discoveries, based on direct experience. In their communion with a higher consciousness they heard a great sound (the *Amen,* some called it; or *AUM,* or *Ahunavar,* or the biblical "sound of many waters"); they beheld an infinite light; they experienced an all-consuming love; above all, they discovered a bliss ineffable. Enlightened souls like these have always urged others to abandon all desires as self-limiting, and to seek transformation in infinite self-awareness.*

The word "religion" derives from the Latin, *religare,* "to tie back, to bind." The "binding" intended here includes various types of *self*-discipline, but is not meant to impose on anyone. A tepid and reluctant populace, unable to accept religion unless it is administered as a kindly admonishment—or else, occasionally, thundered in wrathful anathema!—is not likely in either case to welcome the concept of self-discipline. Institutionalized religion, therefore, does not particularly encourage self-discipline. It enlarges on that concept, rather, by seeking to control the way *others* worship and believe. Indeed, *self*-discipline implies to institutional lead-

*As Saint John of the Cross in Spain put it, "If one desires to become everything, he should desire to be nothing."

ers a certain autonomy, and therefore independence, which might lead in time to heresy.

The truth propounded in the spiritual teachings is not afraid of questioning. Like the sunlight, it simply shines. People who cling forcefully to religious dogmas do so because they lack full confidence in them! They fear to be questioned lest their beliefs—like a snowman under a hot sun—melt shapelessly. Dogmatic religion treads cautiously, as if walking through a dark tunnel, fearful that the candle it holds might be extinguished unexpectedly. Every new idea seems to threaten it, like a fresh breeze which might at any moment make the candlelight flicker and die.

Definitions cannot equal what they define. In religion's firm commitment to its dogmas, so carefully worked out by learned theologians, those definitions seem preferable to reality itself.

At lower levels of religious activity, service is rendered to the public directly. People in the role of serving others may sometimes be aware that a conflict exists between the obedience demanded of them by their superiors and an awareness of the specialized needs of individuals. Perhaps one person needs an answer to some nagging question or doubt. Why, the administrator asks, cannot everyone simply accept the official explanations, so painstakingly worked out for everyone? His preference is for simply announcing the truth, instead of explaining it with careful attention to the wording every time the same subject is raised. This is the particular advantage of dogma: It settles the need for endless further explanations. Administrators, and others in high position, prefer to concentrate on broad policies. Generally, they are impatient with exceptions — particularly with questions that are too reasonable! Policy is their "home ground." It has the same advantage as legal precedents, for it obviates the need to think things through every time anew.

Everything under the sway of duality has its strengths and weaknesses. The need to control people's beliefs is a weakness of religious institutions. It can be neither legislated against nor avoided, since it is simply rooted in human nature. Despite this weakness, however, institutional religion is necessary, and is one of the chief ornaments of civilization. Formal religion helps to raise humanity above the level of the animals, and inspires people to include something nobler in their lives than mere instinctual satisfaction. Institutional religion also, however, in its urge to control, nourishes the craving for power and for the wealth that bestows power. Religion ought to help people out of delusion, but often it manages, by egoic involvement, to steer them back into it again. The theological D.D. degree (Doctor of Divinity) often suggests another meaning to my mind: "Doctor of Delusion."

Religious organizations almost always insist on the importance of obedience. Obedience to whom? Well, since everyone in religion is of course supposed to obey God's will, the only question left is, How to *know* God's will? The authorities answer this question by claiming that it is they themselves who *express* God's will. Many of them, indeed, are more interested in imposing their own will, or perhaps in advancing a purely organizational convenience, than in serving people's personal needs. Rarely do religious authorities express what they call "God's will" in such a way as to demonstrate concern for those needs.

Even when human guidance is offered humbly and sincerely, it is fallible. It may be divinely inspired. Even so, its inspiration must pass through the filter of human understanding. Only one who has attained perfection in God-consciousness can be relied on fully. Such cases, however, are like lonely islands in a vast sea. How should one respond to directives, otherwise, if one considers them unreasonable, or even unrighteous? The wisest of unenlightened human beings can make mistakes.

Two essentials in human interaction are

courtesy and respect. These qualities, like lubricating oil, keep the machinery of human relations running smoothly. Self-righteous or angry confrontation always leaves a residue of negative vibrations, even when the motives are sound, and even when the displeasure is justified. In any disagreement, particularly with one's religious superiors, one should take care to express oneself sincerely and kindly. Never brandish your feelings emotionally, but try to be charitable. Charity is God's way. If you find yourself in disagreement with someone, then, be as much concerned for that person's feelings as for your own. Try to see all people equally as your brothers and sisters in God. Reflect that your superiors, too, are probably only doing their best, according to their own understanding. With a little kindness on your part, you may find it possible to reach some sort of accommodation.

If those attempts fail, however, turn within, and try to deepen your inner relationship with God. Remember, perfection does not exist in this world. Even if some better planet should be discovered somewhere in space—as may well happen someday—the roots of suffering will be found there also, in the contractiveness of ego-consciousness.

There is a third way for resolving conflict:

Withdraw, simply. Go off and live alone with God. For God alone understands you perfectly. If you fear having to support yourself in a life of prayer and meditation — an uneasiness that might well affect you if you've spent your whole adult life serving in an institution — reflect that the Lord is the Sustainer of the universe. If one seeks Him sincerely, he will always be provided for.

Bear in mind, however, that going off on your own will deprive you at least of your present spiritual companions. Everything in life is a compromise. Ask yourself whether living under inept, or even unworthy, authority is not adequately compensated for by that good company. If the alternative to your present situation is to return to a worldly environment, your spiritual quest may suffer a setback. Have you the strength, spiritually, to stand alone? For most people, environment is stronger than will power. Until milk has been churned to butter, it will not float on water. As long as it has the consistency of milk, the water will dilute it. The "milk" of your discrimination, similarly, must be churned by long spiritual practice before it can remain unaffected by worldly influences.

Those, on the other hand, who run religious organizations need to realize that theirs is a stewardship. Their own inner peace will hold them accountable for how they treat others. Unfortunately, high position can breed arrogance. Leaders are not always compassionate toward the needs of others, especially if those others have unconventional opinions regarding dogma or policy. Authoritarian leaders usually oppose change, even when good. They dislike it on principle, as a potential menace to the established order of things, and also to their own position in that order. The wise leader, by contrast, leaves room for reasonable departures from that norm. His outlook is qualitative, not quantitative. It is usual, however, for administrators to think quantitatively. Their attitude obstructs the efforts of sincere seekers, who need *qualitative* guidance.

People often assume, mistakenly, that high position in a religious organization is automatically accompanied by deep spiritual understanding. Rarely is this blithe fancy supported by the facts. Instead, religious institutions tend to become top-heavy with administrators whose gift is for efficiency. Deep spirituality may even be treated at last with a certain smiling condescension, as those in charge become wedded to efficiency, and as their emphasis shifts away, consequently, from the organization's original ideals. The growing concern they show with the mechanics of administration is easily explained: A spreading mission needs workers. Particularly, it needs people with practical skills. The qualifications for administrative positions, then, are no longer limited to spiritual sincerity, but include also efficiency. Few people combine in themselves both qualities. Compromise, sometimes, is therefore necessary. If one candidate for a position is deeply spiritual, but lacks practicality, and another is efficient but not deeply centered in spiritual practices, and if no other candidate is available, the appointment may have to go to the efficient one. That person, in turn, along with others who are selected for the same reason, will feel naturally attracted to people like himself: people who are efficient, rather than spiritual. He and those like him may even tend to avoid those who are more spiritual for the inconvenient reminder they give of the words of Christ in the Book of Revelation: "I know thy works. . . . Nevertheless I have somewhat against thee, because thou hast left thy first love."* Thus, as I said, for purely practical reasons institutions tend in time to become top-heavy with pragmatists.

It would be unfair to blame anyone for this state of affairs. It is simply the way things are,

---

*Revelation 2:2,4.

and the way people are. Religious institutions are not abstractions. They must be run by human beings, and must go along with human nature as it is. Nevertheless, it takes constant individual spiritual effort, inspired from within, to prevent religion from becoming moribund.

Tukaram, a poet-saint in India during the seventeenth century, was employed when young as an accountant. He had deep love for God, and often covered the margins of his ledger-book with spiritual poems, composed by him during his working hours. He became in time one of the brilliant stars in the firmament of India's spiritual history. He was no such star, however, in the eyes of his employer, who finally dismissed him from his job.

A weakness in most religious institutions is the tendency to develop goals other than the quest for truth. Efficiency is one such goal. Power and wealth are others. Indeed, the usual inclination of those running religious organizations is to consider what they say and do to be God's will. The sincere seeker, however, should never take any statement or decision blindly. He should at least try to learn from it. Unquestioning acceptance breeds, not faith, but fanaticism. One should at least question his own understanding. Blind acceptance, especially if contradicted by intuition, though it is often recommended by authorities as evidence of faith, is more usually in fact a sign of unwillingness to shoulder personal responsibility.

Most of those in charge of different aspects of a religious institution are not concerned so much with personal spiritual growth, which to them is a vague issue, as with practical needs. The first concern of the individual, on the other hand, should be with his own relationship with God. He should carefully observe every thought and attitude, correct it when necessary, and probe the self-justifications that rise in the mind to see that they are not mere rationalizations, wearing the mask of righteousness.

Of all the branches of civilization, institutional religion is usually the least adaptable to change. Tradition, not a willingness to consider things on their own merits, is what decides most of its deliberations. The spiritual seeker, however, faces many challenges in his inner search. These demand of him creativity, adaptability, and complete self-honesty. The tests he undergoes cannot be dismissed with ill-considered quotations. The heritage of the past must be balanced against actual, present needs. For the directors of an institution, precedent is sacrosanct. Not so for the sincere spiritual aspirant. For him, truth, not dogma, is the *only* "precedent" worth considering. The divine will, though rooted in eternal truth, is also creative. In confronting difficulties, therefore, it is adaptable. Like waves on the sea, its manifestations — as opposed to its eternal reality — are never fixed and unmoving. Our own approach to truth too, therefore, must be determined by whether we are trudging over a barren desert of material desires, or wading through floods of emotional fervor — the common symptom of foolish causes.

Religious institutions value humility, as do all people of sensitive nature. Too often, however, the particular reason institutions prize humility is for the reassurance it gives them of people's obedience. Wisdom is not interested in such self-serving appreciation. It asks of humility that it strive for perfection in the ego's dissolution in infinite self-awareness. The attitude of religious institutions is, as a rule, less exalted. For one thing, they are not happy with what bodes, to them, the future loss of the right to control.

The spiritual seeker may sometimes have therefore to face in himself the issue of authority. I touched on an aspect of this question earlier. Seekers should ask themselves, How important is outer authority to my quest for God? To what extent does it really entitle anyone to control others? The Lord Himself never imposes on man's free will. Should any human so impose? It would be naive to imagine that every religious superior is highly advanced, spiritually. Sometimes, indeed, the lowliest beggar may be closer to God than many an exalted bishop.

The solution to the dilemma of how to accept religious authority was provided by Jesus Christ. When the Pharisees challenged him for asserting that the divine will should be our guide, he answered, "Render unto Caesar the things that are Caesar's, and unto God the things that are of God." One's inner life is a sacred trust between himself and God. There is no spiritual obligation for him to reveal that life to anyone else. If he is so fortunate as to have someone to guide him who is truly wise, the matter changes for him. He himself would be wise, in that case, to give full confidence, in God's name, to that person. Otherwise, obedience to his religious superiors might be compared to the foreign servitude of the Jews under the Pharaoh of Egypt.* Even religious work belongs in a way to "the things that are Caesar's." It should not be considered among the things

*A similar situation was the self-imposed servitude of the Pandavas during their final year of banishment, as described in India's *Mahabharata*. They accepted that indignity in order to reclaim their hereditary rights in the kingdom that much sooner.

"of God" merely because it is commanded in God's name.

Those in positions of authority, too, should consider above all their inner relationship with God. That should have precedence over all other considerations. A danger of high position is the temptation of imagining that wisdom goes automatically with that position. One may even feel a need to *pretend* wisdom, for fear of losing face. Sincerity may indeed cause him to "lose face," occasionally. At least it will prevent him from falling on it! But what is "face," anyway, to the sincere servant of God? His goal is to serve God, not man. Every worker in the cause of religion would do well to bear in mind the caution Saint Odo of Cluny gave: "The floors of hell are paved with the bald pates of clergymen." High position should be a reminder that food grows more abundantly in the valleys than on the heights. If a leader has true respect for his position, he should take it as God's call to him to give others spiritual nourishment. He should also keep in mind that he is only human, and fallible. It is not necessary that he be always right. He has only to do his sincere best to express God's will. And his guideline in that effort should be his inner peace. The more his actions become attuned to the divine will, the more centered he will find himself in that peace. If once that peace becomes disturbed, however, let him immediately seek the reason for that agitation in himself. Never will the actual cause of it be found elsewhere.

In working with others, all should remind themselves constantly that their true duty is to serve God. The actual beneficiary of that service, moreover, is ultimately the *individual,* not an amorphous mass of people. What is even society but an aggregate of individuals? Though religion is designed for the upliftment of many, it is, in the end, the individual who benefits from its every worthwhile activity. No matter how we define that activity, the gain from it is in *consciousness,* not in the number of people involved. And any upliftment of consciousness, no matter how many it includes, is subjective. One *true* soul, I often say, is preferable in God's eyes to a crowd; and best of all are crowds of souls. There is no gain, as far as God is concerned, from a growing congregation! It is man himself, in consciousness, who gains by his inward transformation. The motto of every religion should be, "Love God, for He is Bliss!" Too often, in contradiction of God's own ways, the unwritten motto is, "Control others in God's name," or, "Control them, lest they offend God." Love between the Creator and His creation should be spontaneous. And in spontaneity, love *becomes* bliss.

Religious organizations are a mixed blessing—a necessary evil: evil, because too often they obstruct people in their search for truth; and necessary, because few people, without religion, would be inspired to seek truth at all.

Beehives are necessary for the accumulation of honey. Religious organizations are necessary for a similar reason: They can accumulate the honey of God's love. Producing and gathering that spiritual honey is the first duty of religion. The sweetness of devotion is no mere sentiment, tearfully expressed: It is heartfelt dedication to attaining truth and bliss. Unfortunately, the organizational "hive" too often becomes the entire goal of people's activity. Will honey accumulate automatically in a hive? It takes a great deal of work on the part of many bees. When the honey of devotion is forgotten in an institution, the institution itself becomes a lifeless shell. High principles should never be subordinated to pressing, but ephemeral, needs. Bliss is the goal: All else is evanescent. After scripture itself becomes dust, what endures is eternal, ever-new, ever-conscious bliss: *Satchidananda.*

People often consider it the aim of religious activity to please God. Why should God want to be pleased? Bliss doesn't fluctuate even when universes spring into existence, or are destroyed! How can anything done by man affect that absolute bliss-consciousness? God is *always* pleased! It is man himself—that is to say, God's presence *within* man—who needs to be pleased by his increasing inner bliss.

Living for God then, is obviously not a dirge chanted in dread of eternal punishment! It ought to be a celebration of eventual victory over every sorrow! The spiritual life, when rightly lived, becomes the funeral of all sorrows. When one is focused too narrowly on rules and restrictions, he becomes guilt-ridden. Obedience should have no other motive than the eventual attainment of bliss. The more conscious one is of his desire for bliss, the greater is his sense of inner freedom.

To be sincere with oneself means not to let his happiness depend on the approval of others. In the context of the quest for bliss, opinions simply do not matter. The only important thing is how to deepen that bliss, and how to spurn any action that obscures it. The judgments of most people are unreliable. Usually they are wrong, because influenced by delusion!

There is a story about a peasant who set out from home, accompanied by his young son, to sell a donkey at a fair. Because he hoped to get the best possible price for the beast, he and the boy walked. The donkey, meanwhile, trotted merrily along, happy for a change to be without any burden to carry.

They'd gone a little distance when they met another group coming the other way. One person in this group burst out laughing. "Just look at that stalwart animal," he cried, "trotting along while those two silly bumpkins trudge wearily at its side. Why don't they ride it?"

The peasant overheard this comment, and thought, "Well, I suppose it does look a bit strange!" He climbed up onto the donkey's back, accordingly, leaving his son to go on by foot.

Some distance further they passed another group, from which a voice rose in outraged protest. "What arrogance!" it cried. "See that grand fellow, seated proudly astride his donkey while his poor child goes limping along in the dust!"

The peasant overheard this comment also, and thought, "Well, I don't want people thinking me arrogant!" Down he got, therefore, and placed his child on the donkey's back instead.

They passed a third group. One person in it covered his mouth as if to show tact, though he was speaking quite loudly enough to be heard outside the group. "What a comedy!" he guffawed. "See that little fellow, in the glory of his youth, ensconced there like a king while his poor old dad hobbles along, trying his best to keep up! Imagine the paucity of discipline in *that* household!"

Well, the peasant didn't know the meaning of "paucity," but he got the general idea. "I don't want to be considered a nobody in my own home!" he thought. Hastily, therefore, he clambered up behind his son. And so they continued, only the donkey now going by foot—or, more correctly, by hoof.

They passed a fourth group. Suddenly there came a stifled cry of horror, "Oh! what heartlessness! Such a heavy load on one poor creature's back! How can they be so unkind to their faithful servant—yes, their *friend!* Ah, how painful, to see such ingratitude!"

At this point the travelers found themselves on a bridge that crossed over a river. The peasant, reflecting that by now he'd been criticized for every possible choice he made, dismounted the donkey in disgust, lifted his son down, and pushed the animal into the water below. And so the two of them returned home, empty-handed.

The moral of this story is, of course, that one should not care excessively about others people's opinions.* Where the quest is for

*What, dear reader, was your own reaction to the end of this

bliss, especially, one must decide for himself what course he will follow, then stick to it unswervingly.

Dear reader, I offer this counsel for you personally. Let others urge you to follow whatever course they like. Good advice, of course, should always be heeded. Above all, however, be guided by your own desire for freedom and inner bliss.

Religion should be a binding to right action— that is to say, to actions that lead to permanent bliss. Don't worry if family, friends, or society disapprove. Social approval is as inconstant as the April breezes! Wait not for the endorsement of others. Don't hesitate to ask their *opinions*— as only opinions, however. Seek endorsement, finally, in your own self.

Don't expect any religious institution, moreover, to do the binding for you. Commit yourself to virtue as a deliberate, personal choice, then adhere to it firmly and joyfully.

Above all, focus your sights on eternity. Treat the passing scene with tolerance, even with amusement. It was created for your and for everyone's entertainment and instruction. It

---

story? Did you join the chorus of critics because of the way the peasant treated his donkey at last? Perhaps the story was meant to test *you!* Can we not suppose the donkey swam away happily, delighted with its new freedom?

isn't God who makes people err! Who does, then—Satan? Don't evade *your own responsibility!* Whatever role Satan plays in your deception, it begins with *your own self! You alone* invite him by your fascination with delusion. Your very connivance is what draws you into that vortex.

Don't hope for wisdom to come to you merely with advancing age. There are many foolish dotards smiling vacantly at the game of life in which they no longer participate. Wisdom comes only by living life in constant watchfulness to see which activities lead truly to happiness, and which only promise happiness, but bring disillusionment and sorrow in the end. Indeed, the only virtue old age demonstrates is the ability, so far, to have refrained from dying!

Grieve not when this dream-universe disappoints you. The disappointment itself is but a dream. Smile joyfully, rather, knowing that the show will end for you at last, and will bring you final victory: the eternal freedom of conscious bliss!

CHAPTER EIGHT

The Refinement of Awareness

If God is for everyone, why isn't religion, which is designed to attract the many, better adapted than the spiritual path to everyone's seeking Him? The answer is that popularity is not the issue. The spiritual path is for those who seek God conscientiously, and who want to do more than merely worship Him: They want to *experience* Him, to love Him. The clergy love such awe-inspiring expressions as, "Almighty Beneficence!" "Supreme Omniscience!" "Omnipotent Ruler of the universe!" They wave incense, clang and toll bells, and intone solemn chants in words that to most people are incomprehensible. A priest in India once told me why it is necessary to make all that noise. "God is deaf," he explained. "We must make a lot of noise to get His attention!"

Formal religion doesn't offer the simple concept of God proposed in this book. Everyone wants bliss, but most people imagine bliss as a kind of outward happiness. God is for everyone, but the real question is, Is everyone for God? Religion itself, as it is commonly taught, promises happiness (again, outwardly) in heaven. Religion is a steppingstone to perfect awareness, but spirituality bridges the whole stream.

All through the soul's long journey away (apparently) from God, its one abiding reality is the consciousness it has of individuality. Only the Self exists. When Conscious Bliss created the universe, it *projected* its own consciousness. In so doing, it assumed an infinity of points of awareness, like little reflections of sunlight scintillating in slivers of glass. The soul is individualized Spirit; in our true nature, therefore, we *are* bliss. Our egos are manifestations of that bliss. Because the ego's attention is outward, however, it doesn't often *experience* more than glimmers of bliss.

From seemingly inanimate matter to dynamic life, everything expresses God. Jagadis Chandra Bose, the great Indian physicist, discovered by experiment that so-called inanimate substances responded to stimuli in much the way that living tissues do. In his speech at the dedication of the Bose Research Institute, which he founded in Calcutta in 1917 — he received knighthood that same year — he described the results of his experiments:

"A universal reaction seemed to bring metal,

plant, and animal under a common law. They all exhibited the same phenomena of fatigue and depression with possibilities of recovery and exaltation, as well as the permanent irresponsiveness associated with death."* Reactions of fatigue and depression are, like suffering and happiness, subjective. They could not exist without consciousness.†

The average person defines himself as his ego, by which he judges everything else. If told that his ego is a delusion, he protests, "It can't be! Don't I know *my own self?* I am, myself, this body and personality!" Ego-centeredness is perfectly understandable given the fact that the average person's experience of life is limited by his ego. Even science accepts that self-awareness begins with the physical body. This is also,

---

*Quoted from *Autobiography of a Yogi,* p. 68 first (1946) edition. This edition is available from Crystal Clarity Publishers, Nevada City, California 95959, U.S.A. – *JDW*

†Other scientists since 1920, when this book was first written and published, have made similar discoveries. Well known among them was the German chemist Karl Friedrich Bonhoeffer. To most of those men, the striking similarities between living and inert matter proved that life and consciousness are nothing but chemical interactions. Surely it is quite as reasonable, however (and certainly more convincing, considering that it takes consciousness to make this assumption!), to explain the similarity between living tissues and inert matter as proof that consciousness, and not chemistry, is the essence of reality. —*JDW*

with modifications, the view of most religionists. For although they distinguish between body and soul, they generally believe that the soul, too, has a form of some kind. They claim that man, although made by God, is *in essence* different from Him. Orthodox Christianity makes a further distinction between ordinary mankind and Jesus Christ. The Nicene Creed states that Christ was "begotten, not made."

Self-realized masters in every age have explained truth as they have actually experienced it. Their explanations in all fundamental matters are unanimous. In the present case, those explanations are very different from the common opinion, taken from the point of view of the ego. Using reason only as a means of explaining to others their own deep soul-perceptions, those masters have shown how illogical it is to believe in a separation between soul, ego, body, and Absolute Spirit. Originally, they explain, there was only the Absolute Spirit. Stars, stardust, planets, oceans, continents, and all living beings were manifestations of that one consciousness. Surely, no other explanation is remotely plausible. From what else could anything have been created? There was only the Spirit's consciousness. A simple way of explaining cosmic creation is to say God *dreamed* the universe.

It would be an error, however, to say that the universe does not exist. The cosmos is not a fiction. Certain pretenders to philosophic wisdom in India have occasionally claimed (misinterpreting their own scriptures) that nothing is real, and that therefore there is no reason to live by any rule of right conduct. "It's all unreal anyway!" they declare with a bland smile. To them who seek this self-deluding excuse for irresponsible behavior I say, "If you really believe everything to be unreal, try eating hot nails or jumping off a tall building!" Everything most certainly is real! It is simply not real *as it appears to be* to the senses. It is real, in other words, *as dreams are real: as a projection of consciousness.* If in your own dream you hit your head against a brick wall, your dream head will hurt!

Western philosophers have long toyed with the concept of consciousness as the underlying reality of everything. Some have proposed a theory called "solipsism," which holds that only the ego-self can be known. The fallacy of this theory is that when the ego is traced to its source, it ceases to exist, as ego! The Self never ceases to be, but that Self is not the ego-self. The soul is a reflection of God; it is individualized Spirit. The problem with seeking truth by reason alone, instead of by direct experience, is that the power of reasoning cannot take one to this deep realization.

There is the more sophisticated belief, also, that everything exists *as mind.* Philosophers faced a problem also with this concept, for they hadn't the firm evidence that would have made it possible for them to work with it. Their methodology precluded their trying to refine their own consciousness rather than depending on the restrictions of reason.

Early in the twentieth century, a solution was found which reason could accept. Science discovered — experimentally — that matter is only a vibration of energy. Sir James Jeans, the eminent British physicist, stated further that the universe looks "suspiciously" — as he put it — like "mind stuff." Since matter is vibrating energy, Jeans was saying that energy itself may be nothing but *a vibration of consciousness.*

Such was in fact the insight expressed thousands of years ago in the writings of India. Modern science has but corroborated that insight. Much modern knowledge, indeed, is not new, but is only a rediscovery of what was known before. The ancient Greeks knew, for example, that the earth is round, and that it is not at the center of everything. The ancient calendar of the Mayas, in central America, was more exact than the modern calendar. And the writings of ancient India indicated sophisticated knowledge of the cosmos, including the following statement: "There are vast worlds all placed within the hollows of each atom, multifarious as the motes in a sunbeam."*

The Absolute, it was explained in India's writings, projected everything *in consciousness.* The first stage in this manifestation was as a universe of ideas. (This stage of manifestation might be compared to an architect's blueprint for a building.) Those thoughts, or ideas, were then vibrated more densely as energy. (This stage resembles the crystallized mental picture the builder has of the finally completed edifice.) Finally, energy was vibrated even more densely, to take the appearance of solid, liquid, and gaseous forms.

Life was never *created:* It produced itself. Consciousness as well as life grew outward from living, conscious centers. Once the material conditions for its manifestation were right, life and consciousness appeared. They were latent from the beginning, in every rock. What rocks we see in our dreams, similarly, are formed by our own consciousness. Were we inclined to do so, we might make those rocks vibrant with life and consciousness. Since we've dreamed them as rocks, however, we probably

* *Yoga Vishishta.*

give them the same rocklike appearance they offer in this greater dream of God's.

In the cosmic dream, when minerals (which derive from the rocks) unite and are quickened as physical bodies, life appears. Increasingly, with progressive evolution, it expresses consciousness. And as the awareness of living creatures grows, it comes at last, in mankind, to manifest *self*-awareness.

The Spirit didn't create as human beings do —for example, when we make a piece of furniture. It had nothing out of which to make anything. What it did was radiate outward from projected centers of living consciousness everywhere. Vibratory movement throughout the universe expanded from those centers. Manifested everywhere to varying degrees is the one, never-changing bliss.

Simply put, then: *Spirit is center everywhere, circumference nowhere.*

The Spirit of God dreamed everything into existence. That "everything" includes our own egos. Awareness expanded outward from that infinity of central points. In evolution's slow ascent toward absolute self-awareness, forms increasingly manifested an already-existing life and consciousness.

The ego's self-awareness may be compared to a reflected image of the moon in a pot filled with water. If there were many such pots, each one filled with water, the reflected images would appear separate and distinct from one another, and also from their source in the moon.

This analogy needs to be further clarified by adding another one, for the reflections of the moon are all identical, whereas human beings are infinite in their variety. Not even two thumbprints are exactly alike. Let us visualize, then, jets of flame projecting from a gas burner on a stovetop. Each jet can be given a distinct appearance by the size of its opening, and by the addition of chemical coloring.

Human egos, like those moon images in pots of water, all reflect the one consciousness of Spirit. Again, like those jets of flame on a gas burner, they are varied *projections* of infinite consciousness. The ego, focused as it is on one body and personality, mistakes that apparently separate individuality for its true self. In reality, selfhood is infinitely greater.

The delusion of ego is dispelled when the soul wakes in infinity. Thus our own dreams, too, disappear when we awake from subconscious sleep. Self-awareness is not obliterated, nor is it submerged, in divine wakefulness: It is simply *expanded to infinity.*

Certain aspects of our own ego-dream can be changed by altering the way we think. For example, when we are ill we can make a strong affirmation of good health and become well again. It is more difficult to change things in the larger dream, but even such a change is not impossible. To effect it, one must attune himself to the Cosmic Dreamer's consciousness. This is what God-realized masters do when they perform what unenlightened people take to be miracles. Because nothing in the universe is fixed permanently, everyone has at least *some* ability to influence the larger dream. As Heraclitus, the ancient Greek, declared, "All is flux." The clearer one is in his own mind, the clearer also can be his effect on the objective world. Thus it is that so-called "primitive" peoples, whose minds are less cluttered by the complexities of "civilization," have been known to change, for example, the weather by the sheer power of concentrated thought.

The evolutionary process is recapitulated in living creatures' growth toward maturity. Physically the process is recapitulated, as we learn in school, with the embryo's development in the womb, where it first manifests lower animal forms, and only at a later stage assumes human shape.

Psychological development is epitomized in people's progress from the passive dependence of a baby on its parents to an adult's assertion of responsibility for the conduct of its affairs.

The ego develops also over successive incarnations. In the process, it repeats ever more clearly the body's development from infancy to physical maturity. For a time, the ego sees itself as wholly dependent on whatever happens to it. Like a baby, its personality lacks definition. Gradually, as it develops, it decides it wants to participate more actively in the events that concern it directly, and seeks within itself the power to influence those events. Thus, it ceases to be a merely passive recipient, and directs its life in ways that it considers more pleasing.

Obviously this development is gradual, not rapid. Psychological maturity could not come with a mere sixty or eighty years of living. Many opportunities are required, many chances to learn and grow, over a succession of bodies if complete psychological and spiritual maturity is even imaginably to be achieved. In the process, one develops increasing awareness of the world around him, awaiting his exploration and discovery. He learns to relate with growing sensitivity to other people. Slowly he overcomes his first sense of helplessness before life's challenges, and develops an inner strength of his own. He comes to see also that other people, and other forms of life, are not very different from himself. He learns to grieve with them in their sorrows and rejoice with them in their joys. Growing empathy loosens the hold egoism has on him: He feels an increasing attunement with life, and senses that a deep unity underlies all existence.

Fairly early in this process of refinement, he develops an urge to express himself creatively: to become a cause in life, not merely an effect. Responding to this urge, he becomes aware, gradually, that a higher consciousness sustains him, reinforces his energy, and even—as he opens himself to it—guides his thoughts. Conscious Bliss, he realizes at last, is the unseen presence behind every experience, even when he sorrows. Thus the ego, at first an important motivator to intelligent action, becomes at last the supreme impediment to attaining bliss.

The ancient Indian teachings gave the first stage of ego-development the name, *tamas,* or *tamo guna.* (*Guna* means quality; *tamas* translates roughly as "mental dullness" and "inertia.") During this stage, the ego submits somewhat passively to whatever circumstances occur. Dull-minded people do not consider themselves responsible for what happens to them, but view it more or less with the resignation most people accord to the weather. Their sense of responsibility increases only gradually, as it does in children.

People with a *tamasic* nature feel no urge to be creatively intelligent. Like pawns in a chess game, they move and act within narrow limits and never consider the possibility that they might, by their own effort, avoid sorrow and attain happiness. Tragedy merely numbs them: It doesn't stir them to deeper understanding. When they suffer, they wish only that other people, or "the authorities," or God Himself would "do something about it." And when things go right, they don't look for reasons to explain their good fortune, in order to keep matters going well in future. They are satisfied, simply, that they've somehow "struck it lucky."

As the ego develops in awareness it begins to wonder if it doesn't have some power of its own to avoid sorrow and find happiness. From passive acceptance, it begins to acquire a more positive outlook. Increasing awareness brings one, in his ascent toward maturity, to the next *guna,* called *rajas. Rajo guna* impels people toward activity.

Tamasic people develop mostly through pain and suffering. They respond not so much reasonably as with emotion. Grieving greatly, but learning little, they are driven haphazardly toward any change that occurs in their lives.

Suffering is the usual prod that life gives people toward higher levels of understanding. As their discernment grows more refined, they understand suffering also in a more refined way. When *tamasic* people begin to look creatively for ways to avoid sorrow and attain happiness, the influence of *rajo guna* appears in them. *Rajasic* people seek above all to fulfill their own ego-generated desires. Intense outward involvement makes them intensely restless. Restlessness, indeed, like a whip, drives them relentlessly through the storms of life. Lashed by their desire to own and control everything they can, *rajasic* people long at last for peace. They arrive, thus, at the third and final stage in their upward climb: *sattwa guna.*

Sattwa develops out of more, however, than the painful recognition of one's need for relief from the hot winds of worldliness. It also comes when one desires inner peace as a positive blessing, not as merely passive relief. This positive desire is the fruit of a gradually expanding understanding.

Tamasic people never introspect, and never even examine things closely. Since mental suffering usually results from disappointed expectations, *tamasic* people suffer only slightly on a mental level. Their suffering is primarily physical in nature. The suffering of *rajasic* people, on the other hand—apart from those ills to which all flesh is heir—is primarily emotional. It includes the agony of a nerve-searing restlessness. For *sattwic* people finally, the keenest suffering results from distress in their conscience.

At all levels of refinement, development can also be inspired by good company. This influence is even more important than suffering. *Tamasic* people, too, can be helped toward spiritual maturity by surrounding them with uplifting influences. Particularly helpful to them is service under persons more highly evolved spiritually than themselves. The *tamasic* person may find it beneficial to work as a servant wherever harmony prevails, or to serve in a supportive capacity under someone of executive, even *rajasic* character. He should be helped to see that service to persons of clearer understanding than himself is not in any way demeaning to him.

The clearer a person's awareness grows, the more rapid his psychological evolution becomes. Good company stimulates that evolution; it balances the whips of pain and suffering, which drive a person toward greater understanding. *Rajasic* people, if they find themselves among peace-loving, harmonious people, can be inspired to recognize that happiness exists in themselves, and needn't be sought only in outer circumstances.

Thus maturity is achieved, ultimately. On

the one hand, the ego is driven forward. On the other hand, it is attracted upward. Good company magnetizes. So also does good action. Suffering, on the other hand, repels one from the behavior that attracted it. The suffering of *rajasic* people is often due to the loss of some prized possession. *Sattwic* people, on the other hand, suffer more in the *excess* of possessions! Even in artistic matters, their taste inclines them to simplicity. *Sattwic* people suffer keenly also if they realize they've offended against some principle — a consideration that has little meaning for most *rajasic* people.

Everybody wants freedom, but the *rajasic* person equates freedom with material security, which the *sattwic* person sees as utterly unstable. *Rajasic* people think to find security in a large bank account, and in worldly prosperity. *Sattwic* people seek security, rather, in themselves. They want few possessions, and desire above all to control their own thoughts, emotions, and energies, all of which they direct consciously toward attaining supreme bliss.

Tamasic people never really try to achieve any sort of control. Suffering makes them ask at last, "Why — *Why?*" They begin to wonder, "What can I, myself, do about it?" Thus it is that *rajo guna* begins to manifest in them, and with it the desire to control more and more of their environment. What *rajas* causes, finally, is an overextension of energies. Restlessness robs people of whatever peace and happiness they once knew, perhaps as children. They come in time to realize that the world is simply too vast, and life too fluid, to be controlled by mere human effort.

At this point the ego, instead of continuing to ascend further, may slip backward in rejection of life's challenges altogether, choosing rather the passive "peace" of non-involvement that is *tamo guna*. If, however, the ego decides it wants to continue growing in maturity toward higher awareness, it seeks the positive peace that is *sattwa guna*.

It then discovers, to its happy surprise, that the control it sought when influenced by *rajo guna* comes with little effort or strain by attuning itself to whatever aspect of the dream-reality it wants to express.

The Spirit's way of creating is to *become* whatever it creates. Man, too, by deepening his attunement with the divine spirit within him—with, that is to say, his own higher Self—finds that the process of creativity is simply a matter of *becoming,* mentally, that which he wants to express. If his intention is to create beautiful music, he needs only to "tune in" to the divine consciousness expressed through music, and uplifting melodies, chords, and rhythms will appear clearly in his mind. That music will of course be filtered by the vibrations of his own consciousness, but it will come from a higher source, and will not be hammered out, so to speak, on a forge by the artifices of his own ego. If he wants to paint or to sculpt beautifully, attunement with the higher consciousness behind color, form, and symmetry gives him the knowledge of how to express those inspirations. And if he wants to manifest material abundance, he has only to develop the *consciousness of abundance* for its material reflection to be attracted to him. Any desire he conceives is like a magnet, attracting success in that field.

This does not mean he has no need for technical skills. Being endowed with a keen conscience—the quality of *sattwa*—he will do his best to achieve perfection outwardly, as he strives to achieve it inwardly. Without inspiration as well, however, material skill is but an empty vessel, lacking the nectar that might quench people's thirst for upliftment.

If once he succeeds in expressing true inspiration, by following the method I suggest, he would be foolish indeed if he sought, or even desired, any personal credit. For he will only have actualized a universal, and essentially quite simple, law.

Each person's destiny is the consequence also of his own actions in the past. He can change much of the destiny that has been set in motion by those actions, however, by raising his present level of consciousness. As he ceases to separate himself mentally from life's larger plan, he begins seeking ways for how Conscious Bliss may want him to contribute toward its unfoldment. Thus, he understands ever more clearly how he might, if it is asked of him, further that plan.

Sattwa means "to elevate, to uplift." The true goal of all upliftment of consciousness is to perceive truth. *Sattwa guna* influences one in ways that *rajasic* people cannot easily comprehend. It makes a person, for one thing, less inclined to see things as involving him personally. This doesn't mean he becomes less loving. It is simply that he feels less motivated by self-interest. The more *sattwa guna* influences him, the less inclined he feels to give much thought to the demands of his own ego. Acclaim by others no longer attracts him, for he no longer defines himself in terms of anything he has done. He seeks, for companions, people whose inclinations are similarly expansive. And he determines to depend no longer on anything outside himself. He understands deeply the purport of Jesus Christ's words at the end of the Sermon on the Mount: "Be ye therefore perfect, even as your Father which is in Heaven is perfect." (Matthew 5:48)

The company a person keeps has a strong influence on the images of happiness he forms in his own mind. If everyone he knows considers it the goal of life to own a large bank account, he will not easily dismiss that thought-form from his mind even if his own desire is to embrace a more expansive ideal. If, on the other hand, the people around one are generously interested in the well-being of others, whatever temptation he feels to seek only his own happiness will be more likely to fade away like morning mist in the sunshine.

Environmental influence is usually stronger than will power. One must have great inner strength to resist it successfully. Milk, as I've said before, mixes with water. It must be churned to butter, first; only then will it float, and not become diluted. Until a person's consciousness has been "churned," similarly, to the "butter" of wisdom by spiritual practices, he must recognize how vitally important it is to associate with people who have the consciousness that he wants to achieve.

In the development toward maturity, one feels an increasing desire for true understanding. Aware at last of how much, and how often, he has erred even though trying his best—for delusion is very subtle—he begins to yearn for the guidance of someone who has himself attained wisdom. It will be his supremely good fortune if he is led to such a person. If, moreover, that person consents to take on the Herculean task of leading him out of the labyrinth of delusion, he will, after great effort also on his own part, attain freedom at last. Without such guidance, the way is endlessly tortuous and, repeatedly, disappointing.

One should bear in mind always that, as long as there is still the possibility of further progress, there remains also that of retrogression. Permanent freedom comes only with complete transcendence of the ego. Transcendence comes alone with final release from the three *gunas*.

That person alone can assume the task of leading others out of delusion who has himself achieved that perfect freedom. It is, in the highest sense, Conscious Bliss itself which sends such free souls to guide others, deeply sincere in their spiritual quest and eager to exchange their narrow ego-identity for one that is infinite.

Ego-transcendence is the final stage of ego-refinement. With it comes the realization that there was, after all, nothing to be transcended! For behind the whole universe, sustaining and inspiring it, is the ever-conscious bliss of *Satchi-dananda*.

Each level of refinement brings the inspirations that are appropriate to it. The inspirations themselves become increasingly subtle. For the *tamasic* person, inspiration means only the stimulation of his animal appetites. For the *rajasic* person, it means emotional excitement, and requires an appeal, usually, to his desire for self-aggrandizement before he'll even consider an attempt at self-betterment. For *rajasic* people to want *sattwic* consciousness, they must be convinced of the superior attractions of *inner* peace and, above all, of bliss.

It is the *sattwic* quality, however, that enables one especially to realize that it is God, truly, who bestows every fulfillment. As *sattwa guna* develops in a person, he feels motivated increasingly *from within*. Consequently, he depends less and less on outer influences. All his thoughts, energies, and desires are directed toward reaching the only lasting reality: Conscious Bliss. This direction of his entire being toward climbing the highest peak of consciousness is the meaning of the biblical statement, which Jesus Christ said is the first commandment: "Thou shalt love the Lord thy God with all thy heart, and with all thy soul, and with all thy mind, and with all thy strength."

CHAPTER NINE

The Return to Zero

Human nature thinks linearly. Progress, to most people, means going *from* something *to* something else: from cause to effect; from youth to old age; from point of departure to point of destination. Man doesn't naturally think that everything exists literally here and now in time and space. He lives *for,* but not *in,* the present moment: not in the changeless NOW, in other words, *behind* the present moment. His gaze is focused on the motion picture screen of life rather than on the changeless present tense in the projection booth, whence issues that complex interplay of shadows, sound, and light.

The ego evolves from lower to higher stages of refinement—from *tamas* to *rajas* to *sattwa*—arriving finally at what in Sanskrit is called *triguna rahitam,* the state beyond the three *gunas* and beyond all vibration. As I hinted toward the end of the last chapter, no actual evolution takes place, for in reality nothing ever changes.

Divine attainment comes not by scaling some high mountain peak, but by flattening out the mountains and valleys of life. An illustration that may clarify this concept better, since the world is constantly in motion, is tossing waves on the sea. The motion of the waves doesn't affect the sea's overall level. Even a hundred-foot wave would not raise that level by one millimeter; the upward surge of that wave would be compensated for elsewhere by a depression.

The ego is one of those countless waves, whereas Conscious Bliss, the unchanging reality, is the vast sea itself. In concentrating on our one wave, we try to give ourselves self-importance by lifting the wave high, thinking even to affect the level of that whole body of water. The sea, however, never changes. We do well, of course, to try generously to improve the quality of life on earth if only because we uplift ourselves by that effort, but if our efforts are directed only toward raising our own wave above the others, we produce in ourselves and in others around us only tension, insecurity, and unhappiness — and then, the inevitable crash. No wave retains its height more than fleetingly. From ancient Egypt, China, and India to the skyscrapers and freeways of modern times the human condition has remained essentially what it always was: rising expectations followed by sinking disappointments.

The secret of fulfillment is to stop trying to become higher, better, more successful than anyone else, and to subside calmly, becoming a little wave, unimportant to ourselves as our wave crest remains close to the bosom of the sea. Egoic ambition creates a desire to pull away from the ocean bosom. Every such effort is, in the words of Shakespeare, "much ado about nothing." It is "a tale told by an idiot, full of sound and fury, signifying nothing."

All spiritual progress is a return, simply, to one's original state, which forever was, and forever will be, for through all eternity it is that which simply IS.

Identification with the body, and our resulting attachment to it, is the root cause of all suffering. Without this hindrance of a limited identity, our happiness would be unalloyed. The earth might have been, for everyone, a paradise had man accepted it as God's dream instead of distorting paradise by trying to make it conform to his own selfish desires. He could have enjoyed the dream, and would not have suffered. Ignorantly, alas, he has brought disorder and confusion to the dream. He might have lived in freedom, like a tourist, wandering about happily and relishing the sights, learning from them, and absorbing every experience as an enrichment of his understanding. At the end of his visit he would have handed in his ticket at the "gate," smiling, and slipped easily away, pleased to be returning home again. Instead, attachment has brought him endless suffering. He clings tenaciously to the things of earth, wanting this, that, and the other thing for his very own. The earth could have been experienced as a Garden of Eden. Instead, he has turned it into a tangled undergrowth, rank with weeds of selfish ambition.

Desire and attachment: These two keep energy flowing ever outward to the senses. Nature Herself counsels an alternative rhythm: action during the daytime, balanced by calm, restful sleep at night. Man, instead, seizes life with both hands, never really resting even when he is asleep. He could have enjoyed life. Instead, happiness itself escapes him like mercury when grasped too tightly in the hand.

Attachment is most strongly expressed in the survival instinct—a reflection, distorted by attachment, of the soul's awareness that it is immortal. Clinging to the body, man fears to lose it, along with all the familiar associations he has built up over a lifetime. His heart pleads with death, "Must all this be really abandoned *forever?*" The *things* themselves must be left behind, yes, but not all the people. Their forms will change, but not their essence. We may find those we love decked out in fresh forms, attracted again by the magnet of mutual love.

Desires are as multifarious as waves on the sea. An instinct all creatures have implanted in them is that of propagating their species. The sexual instinct originally springs from the impulse to affirm one's own continued existence. The effect of this instinct, however, is far-reaching, for people as they grow in refinement seek ever-subtler ways of perpetuating their existence: through works of art, music, or literature, by creating noble works as monuments to their expanding awareness, or by sharing with others whatever wisdom they acquire.

Sexuality, the physical aspect of creativity, causes as much grief as happiness because of the intense attachments it forms. Indeed, all kinds of creativity trail behind them a certain vapor train of disappointment: the thought that, no matter how sincerely one tries, one can never fully express the inspiration he feels in what he does. Even human children, born though they are of a different kind of love, often disappoint the parents who lovingly invite them to share their homes. They come as strangers, often, and may remain strangers to the end.

The ego instinctively seeks its own kind of

immortality, but how little one leaves behind him after death! Everyone has a unique personal destiny to work out. Seldom do people feel obligated or even interested in helping their forebears to work out a different destiny. The hope of finding some kind of immortality through one's descendants is pure fantasy. So far as one's own awareness is concerned, it is not perpetuated through the children of our bodies, nor even through the fruits of one's creative labors. What is the supposed "immortality" of fame? One loses interest in what he has done once he's breathed his last. Mozart's music is loved by thousands today, but is Mozart himself aware of that fame? Even if he is enough evolved spiritually to be conscious of it, he certainly sees it in a broader context now, one that deprives it of any particular personal meaning for him. His real reward has been the joy he felt while composing it, and the lingering effect of that joy on his present consciousness. Whether our deeds remain with us or not, as memories, their real importance, for us, is how they've affected our consciousness.

Life does not cease with the body's death. Self-continuance is nothing we need even worry about: There can never be any threat to it. The soul cannot be destroyed or even slightly disturbed. God Himself could not destroy it.

No matter how many times we err, the soul is immortal, and is a part of God Himself, of Conscious Bliss.

What holds us prisoners to limitation is, above all, the power of desire. The fulfillment of desires causes us as much pain as pleasure, for things we desire have no permanence. The gains and losses of life are self-canceling. They must all, in the end, total zero! For creation itself exists on the principle of duality. Every plus must be balanced by a minus, every gain, canceled out by a loss—even as all the waves are compensated for by corresponding depressions in the sea.

What a supreme irony, that all the struggles, the desires and ambitions, the hopes, the ever-present fear of failure, the careful planning, the investment of years of effort, the sacrificial deferral of fulfillment, the eager longings and expectations—all must lead from any success achieved to "the morning after": cancelation by an equal and opposite failure! Zero cannot but be the sum total. That is the law of the universe. Think of all the tears, the anguish and frustration of waiting, the laughter of relief at reaching eventual success, and all of it, literally, for nothing!

Perfection can be achieved only by subsiding into the oneness of Spirit. What this means for each of us is utter acceptance that change-lessness is our one abiding reality. Instead of trying to lift ourselves up self-importantly, we should accept the simple truth that we are a part of God, and that He is our entire reality. The closer we keep our wave-crest to the bosom of the vast sea, the greater will be our happiness, and the greater also the beauty and inspiration in anything we create.

Desire is simply an affirmation of need. Always it carries with it a certain pain, for awareness of need, is always to some extent painful. Pain accompanies fulfillment also, for the pleasure of fulfillment is only one side of a coin: Pain is the reverse side. People hope, in their pursuit of pleasure, to escape pain, but they fail to realize that the two are a single reality. The more one revels in pleasure, the more he experiences also its opposite pain. These two states swing forever back and forth, left and right, like the movement of a pendulum. The farther the movement in either direction, the farther it must be also in the opposite direction. These are ineluctable facts. Pain and pleasure, sorrow and happiness, grief and delight: these oppositional states belong inextricably together.

What is to be done, then? Duality's movement, like that of a playground swing, can be increased at will or, alternatively, slowed and even stopped. The trick is to resist, mentally, the forward motion toward pleasure, and to withhold one's mind also from the backward movement toward pain. Mental detachment need not result in boredom or apathy, if stillness is understood for itself, and not as a mere alternative to motion. The process of constantly swinging back and forth between laughter and tears creates only emotional agitation. One attains inner joy only in the peace of mental and emotional non-attachment. In inner calmness, not in outer exuberance, Conscious Bliss is attained.

Bliss is the state midway between every pair of opposites. It is the zero point, where all motion ceases. Even in gentle movement long before rest is completely achieved, there is far more happiness than ever comes through excitement. Calm movement has its oppositional states also, but every dip of the wave brings, not sadness, but rather a smile of reflection that bliss is our deepest reality.

Habit is that person behind the swing, pushing it repeatedly toward renewed outwardness. Again and again, habit-driven, people create ever-fresh desires in the hope of satisfying their desire for happiness. Like children laughing with every forward swing, they delight in new sensations, new acquisitions. Even the backward swing toward loss might be, in the release it brings, a cause of happiness if they didn't sicken with it, as children sometimes do, but swung in both directions with non-attachment! Their attachment, however, to specific fulfillments, instead of freely enjoying whatever comes their way, brings them repeated sorrow. Pleasure and displeasure are simply ideas in the mind, which can be changed. It is our expectation of happiness in specific forms that exposes us to unhappiness also. By releasing that expectation, we are never disappointed! Real power resides at the rest point between every oppositional swing. To withdraw mentally from both opposites and live at rest in one's own "zero point" is to become strong in oneself. His strength then brings him a happiness that never comes to those who depend weakly on outward satisfactions. This seeming stoicism brings great inner joy, which is in its own way the opposite of apathy.

Disappointment is always commensurate with the intensity of one's frustrated desire. The farther the swing in any direction, the farther its return in the opposite direction. People who revel in pleasure always suffer from contrasting moods of depression. Any present sad moods they have are the consequence of past sense indulgences. One should resist them. If, instead, he gives in to them, he merely attracts to himself the desire to repeat that indulgence.

What lures people onward is hope. When a fisherman hooks a trout, the fish takes the bait that has been dangled before it, thinking to enjoy this colorful tidbit. The fisherman reels in his fish only a certain distance, then lets it run freely for a time—"playing" it until it tires before reeling it in all the way. Such is the "play" of delusion, once people have swallowed the bait of desire. The time involved in this play with them is, as a rule, longer than the time needed for catching a trout! Because of that longer time span, one doesn't soon perceive delusion for what it is. He may live his whole life in wealth and comfort, though perhaps in questionable honesty, and die peacefully in his bed, leaving behind him what some think of as a glowing success. Death is a convenient, if deceiving, curtain closer. What happens after that is hidden from all but the one who dies. Religion threatens hell for people if they live wrongly here on earth, but what about the *inner* hell some carry about with them all the time?

Look carefully at a baby, and ask yourself: Is it basically happy, or sad? Has its first birth-cry been prolonged in a continuous wail of disappointment? Or do the tears it sheds soon become gurgles of contentment? What do its attitudes suggest of its own past? Granting that there are more immediate explanations also for such attitudes, is there yet a suggestion, here, of some former happiness or regret? This consideration may help those responsible for the child's upbringing. How many dramas may the book of life conceal, if one only knew how to read!

In a cinema love story, the hero and heroine undergo many tribulations. At last they marry to euphoric music. Loved ones smile at them and wish them every happiness. The couple gaze fondly into each other's eyes. Joyfully there flash on the screen the words, "THE END." And the audience goes home reassured that here were two, at least, who lived "happily ever after." The director was clever: He ended the movie at that point. No morning after. No rolling pins and black eyes!

Of course, by no means all weddings end sadly. Enough of them are followed by happy honeymoons and a life of reasonable contentment to keep the myth of conjugal bliss alive. All the same, even happy marriages conceal a certain sadness: the recognition of what a colossal compromise human love is, compared to the soul's longing for perfect love. Human happiness seldom exposes, even to the persons concerned, its hidden disappointments. People usually close out such thoughts, for life's rhythms are long enough to cloud the memory of past sorrows. Always people hope that, somehow, things will "turn out all right."

Thus, the matron whose marriage has been a lifelong disappointment can hardly wait to get the young ladies in her social set married off — not because she wants to inflict misery on them, but because she persuades herself that her own days of humdrum resignation will be different, this time.

And so the myth lives on!

Human happiness is a ripple in the river of time. The little child with shining eyes, sweet laughter, and gentle smile may become, in middle age, a rapacious tycoon. The beautiful maiden with rosy complexion, radiant gaze, and melting looks seems the very essence of loveliness. Can that older woman a few years later — sallow-skinned, dull-eyed, scowling perpetually, her face deeply lined with disillusionment — really be the same human being? The soft sweetness of youth has hardened into cynicism. Which of these two is the real one? The answer is, Neither of them! Change blows over a person's life like a breeze over the surface of a pond. It ruffles the surface of his ego with ripples of pleasure and displeasure, but ever briefly. Nothing lasts. If people die happy they go dancing off the stage to happy, or envious, applause, change their costumes, and re-emerge in other roles—whether happy or sad depending on how well they have acted so far. Nothing ever defines them as they really are. In time, the monotonous repetition causes unspeakable anguish. For one remembers his lost bliss, and cannot but compare his present state to one that might be.

Desire keeps one tied to outwardness as if to a wheel, forever turning. People long to avoid pain permanently and find lasting happiness; the wheel keeps turning, however, and constantly repeats the experience of success and failure. If money fails, or love, or fame, or any other dream, they tell themselves something else will turn up eventually. Or they'll get back in a new form whatever they lost. (How often it happens that people get divorced only to marry others very much like their first mates!) There are enough reasons to keep people hoping they'll find gold at the end of the rainbow to keep them following a constant succession of rainbows to their ever-earthy conclusion for incarnations.

Meanwhile, God says, "I have always loved you! If you wish it, I can go on waiting." He has eternity. So also have we. But is there any sense in spending aeons watching while every fulfillment gets snatched away, each to be replaced by disappointment and suffering? Release can come only when the soul is re-united with God.

The fact that outer happiness is always a precursor to disappointment needn't mean one can never be truly happy in this world. It all depends on how we direct our attention. If we live fully aware that our little wave arose from the sea, and is a part of it, and if therefore we wisely keep the crest of our wave down close to that reality, we can be happy always. Once we learn to attune every thought and action to God's will, and serve others as instruments of His peace, we can live everywhere in inner freedom. Nothing can prevent us, then, from being happy always. Casting out of our hearts every ego-affirming desire, we find ourselves drifting peacefully on refreshing currents of inner bliss.

Accept joyfully, therefore, whatever comes to you. View it as a gift from God. Even persecution and pain can bring blessings of bliss, for they always reveal, in time, a benign purpose. Make bliss your own — whether here on this earth, in some astral heaven, or in infinity. Drink daily at the fountain of inner joy, and bliss will be yours forever.

Jesus Christ put it beautifully: "Seek ye first the kingdom of God, and His righteousness, and all these things shall be added unto you."

CHAPTER TEN

The Science of Religion

Religion in the deeper, spiritual sense is not defined by sentimental flights of poetry, nor by prayers pleadingly offered in wan hope of a response. Rather it is a pragmatic science which gives practical results.

Religious teachings contain lofty sentiments as well. These, cynics often scoff at as maudlin for the fact that they are not merely sentiments, but lofty. The sentiments which those teachings emphasize, however, can be tested and proved. If they give universal, and universally desirable, results, why discount them simply because they promote happiness? Indeed, why for that reason label them unscientific? Widespread human experience is equivalent, in its way, to experiments in the laboratory. If experience demonstrates, for example, that kindness is more effective than selfishness, and not merely useful as a technique of diplomacy, but effective for the fulfillment it gives him who offers it, wouldn't it be foolish to toss the demonstration aside as irrelevant, pragmatically? Jesus Christ said, "It is more blessed to give than to receive." The "blessing" he referred to is reminiscent of *bliss,* which is the theme of this book. The supreme argument against selfishness is that in the long run it simply doesn't work. People who amass fortunes for themselves but never share of that abundance end up feeling soured on life.

The happiness people really want in life is not found in egoic self-absorption, but by expanding the sense of self to embrace others. Generous giving *is* pragmatic, therefore, and not merely a dogmatic precept. The blessing brought by generosity is a reality one discovers in consciousness, not with test tubes or telescopes. In that realm it gives definite, *desirable* results.

It is a *religious* discovery also, for sharing with others in God's name makes one more aware of God's presence everywhere.

There is another aspect of scientific religion, however, which is quite independent of anything done in God's name. Its results, too, are specific, and don't require support from any system of belief. It is based on observation, and on the *actual experience* of concrete realities. It includes the *feeling* aspect of consciousness, which is centered in the heart.

The feeling aspect is one of the four aspects of consciousness, all of them with their corresponding centers in the body. The intellect is centered in the forehead, between the eyebrows. The ego is centered in the medulla oblongata, at the base of the skull. The mind in its perceiving, pre-discriminating aspect, radiates outward from the top of the head.

In 1917 I asked Sir Manindra Chandra Nundy, the Maharajah of Kasimbazar, to consider sponsoring my work. At the time I planned to offer boys an all-rounded education: physical, mental, and spiritual. The maharajah decided to test my fitness as a teacher of spiritual truths. To this end, he summoned a group of pundits, or scriptural scholars, to subject me to an examination. I could see the moment I entered the room that they were ready for a theological bullfight! My own approach to truth is experiential, not scholarly. I decided, therefore, to seize the initiative by examining *them!* After a momentary, inward prayer for guidance, I said to them, "Let us limit this discussion to what we've actually *experienced* of scriptural truths." This was, I knew, an aspect of the subject to which they were strangers, even though the scriptures themselves insist on one's need to *realize* the truth. I then posed them a question to which I knew they wouldn't have the answer.

"The scriptures tell us," I said, "that consciousness has four aspects: *mon* [mind], *buddhi* [intellect], *ahankara* [ego], and *chittwa* [feeling].* They also tell us that these four have their corresponding centers in the body. Can any of you tell where those centers are located?"

Well, they couldn't answer. The scriptures themselves, you see, are silent on the point! I then gave them the above explanation: *Mon,* I told them, is at the top of the head; *buddhi* is at the point between the eyebrows (the *ajna chakra* as it is called); *ahankara* is in the medulla oblongata; and *chittwa* is centered in the heart. There was no further discussion! The maharajah was happy to sponsor my school.

Notice how, when a person thinks deeply, he tends to knit his eyebrows. If he allows praise to "go to his head," he'll draw his head back in the universal posture of pride. When first he becomes aware of something, before discerning what it is, his awareness withdraws a little to the middle of his brain, the center of which is at the top of the head. And when he feels something deeply, he may even put one or both hands to his chest over the heart, for this

---

Chittwa means the feeling aspect of consciousness. Most scholars are not clear on this word, explaining it vaguely in such terms as, "consciousness in its lower aspects," or, even more vaguely, as, "mind stuff."

is where his feelings are centered. When feeling is emotional, it radiates outward from that center. When it is intuitive, it withdraws to its own center. Here in the heart are generated a person's likes and dislikes, his desires and aversions.

The frontal lobe of the brain, anatomically speaking, is our most recent acquisition. This is the focus of the higher aspects of consciousness, including the intellect. Notice how, by contrast, the foreheads of lower animals slope sharply backward. The seat of the intellect is, as I've indicated, just behind the forehead at a point midway between the eyebrows. Only human beings have access to the higher aspects of consciousness, including not only the intellect, but also the will power, concentration, and super-consciousness. The ancient teachings described this as the seat of spiritual vision, calling it "the spiritual eye." By deep concentration at this point, all the higher faculties are stimulated.

The heart center, or *anahat chakra,* is in the dorsal plexus of the spine, just behind the heart. This is, as I said, the center of feeling in both its emotional and intuitive aspects. Intuitive feeling includes spiritual love and devotion, without which aspiration itself remains an abstraction. A disappointed lover may lament, "My heart feels broken!" He will never express his pain by crying, "My knee hurts!" Devotion can be developed by awakening the heart's energy. Vague efforts to awaken it by prayer alone are far less effective.

The spinal energy flows in two directions: up, toward the brain; and down, toward the base of the spine. When the upward flow is the stronger, one's consciousness rises also and produces a happy, positive outlook. Thus, an interrelationship exists between the directional flow of energy and that of consciousness. The energy-flow is controlled by feeling in the heart. Positive feelings direct that flow upward; negative feelings direct it downward. When the energy flows upward, it inspires happiness. That direction is first generated, however, by the *desire* to be happy. Desires, plus energy, produce will power. The will directs the energy to flow either upward or downward depending on whether the desire directing it is positive or negative. The energy-flow *facilitates,* without defining, the direction of consciousness. Even so, an upward flow of energy increases the feeling of happiness. First, then, must come the mental predisposition to be happy.

A downward flow of energy, on the other hand, is produced primarily by depressed feeling, but it also increases the intensity of those feelings. A number of physical factors can draw the energy downward also, and may in their turn·draw the consciousness downward also if the will is not resistant to that direction. Toxins in the lower bowels, for instance, can draw the energy downward, exacerbating one's negative feelings if he has the slightest tendency to feel depressed already.

People everywhere on earth, regardless of any expectation based on belief, are to some extent conscious of these movements. They may not be sensitively aware of the energy flowing in the spine, but they are familiar with "that bubbly mood," and with "that sinking feeling." When they are happy, they may exclaim "I feel high," or, "I'm feeling uplifted." When they are sad, they may complain, "I feel downcast," or, "I'm rather low today."

Popular fancy locates heaven above us in the sky, and hell below us inside the earth. The simple facts, objectively considered, offer no support for these concepts. No telescope has ever revealed angels flitting about in outer space; nor has any up-to-date mining method raised demons in angry protest on an oil gusher. What is "up" for us is "down" for the people on the other side of the earth. Obviously, then, heaven and hell are not literally above and below us. Nevertheless, the popular fancy should not be dismissed as a superstition. What it actually describes are two directions of energy *in the body*. Every language must contain comparable expressions, reflecting these universal realities.

Posture, too, affects the energy movements in the spine. A person who is unhappy sits slumped forward, walks heavily on his heels, hangs his head, and looks naturally downward. The corners of his mouth turn down, and his lower eyelids sag revealing white below the iris. When one is happy, on the other hand, he sits up straight, walks and stands with his weight lightly on the balls of his feet, holds his head up, and gazes more naturally straight ahead, or even upward. His mouth curves up, and his lower eyelids rise slightly, perhaps touching the iris, in an alert attitude.

People who slump forward, gaze habitually downward, and display other physical signs of depression, are not likely to exclaim, "I'm wonderfully happy!" Nor do they walk jauntily, keep their heads up, curve their mouths upward in a smile, or gaze level with the ground, or upward (except, possibly, in truculent challenge!). It would require an act of will to contradict these natural tendencies, which have nothing to do with social conditioning or with any religious belief. They do in fact, however, correlate with spiritual *experience*.

There is another link between the body and

the feeling quality. When a person is happy he naturally fills his lungs with air, as if to affirm his enjoyment of life. By contrast, when one is unhappy he tends to breathe shallowly — except, indeed, in preparation for a heavy sigh. Shallow breathing suggests a desire to have as little to do with the world as possible. Normally, when one is unhappy, his exhalation becomes stronger. When, conversely, his feelings are "up," his inhalation is stronger than his exhalation.

The breath is not only a mechanism for bringing oxygen into the body and for expelling from it carbon dioxide. It interrelates with the flow of energy in the spine, and affects thereby a person's state of consciousness. With inhalation, the energy rises; with exhalation, it descends. Indeed, on a subtler level the energy-flow *produces* the physical breath. Thus, there is a reciprocity between the two. Happiness draws the energy upward, and strengthens the inhalation. One can also raise his energy, and achieve greater mental upliftment, by simply inhaling deeply. The opposite is as true: A sigh not only *expresses* sadness: It can also *induce* it.

These are objective facts. They don't depend on any belief, religious or other, but are a simple manifestation of universal realities. They do, however, correlate with religious *teachings,* inasmuch as they influence one's state of consciousness.

In many religions, certain aware persons have explored these realities to enhance their spiritual practices. By sensitive application, these facts have been developed into an actual *science of religion*. Such, indeed, is the basis of the great science presented to the world in the nineteenth century by Lahiri Mahasaya of Benares, India, who resurrected it from ancient times and gave it the unpretentious name, Kriya Yoga. *Kriya,* in Sanskrit, means *action*. Kriya Yoga is a particular kind of action or technique that draws on universal, central, and to some extent commonly known facts of human nature.

The Christian Hesychasts of Greece, centuries ago, drew on these facts when they counseled that the recitation of the well-known prayer, "Lord Jesus Christ have mercy on us," should be uttered in conjunction with the breath. The first three words, they said, should be uttered while inhaling, and the next four, "have mercy on us," while exhaling. The first part of the formula is an appeal. It is therefore offered up to Christ and to the superconscious with the upward-flowing energy. The last part is a request to *receive* grace into the body and into one's self. It therefore accompanies the downward-flowing energy with exhalation, as if seeking to bring grace down to oneself. It is noteworthy that in this practice the upward- and downward-flowing energies are not associated with thoughts of happiness and sadness. Thus, we see that those moods are simply *examples* of the effect of the upward and downward movements of energy.

In Kriya Yoga also, the rising and descending energies in the spine are not expected to make the practicant alternately happy and sad, but to make him increasingly aware, rather, that he himself is the source, indeed the controller, of every like and dislike. Centering those reactions in himself rather than in outer circumstances, he brings his very awareness to a center within himself. No longer does his "zero point" signify, for him, a cancelation of outward-directed reactions: It becomes a cancelation in the deeper sense of nullifying his separation from the Infinite Spirit. The upward flow, then, becomes an act of total worship, and the downward flow, a withdrawing more and more deeply into his inner self. The dual flow of energy finally so magnetizes the spine that the flow enters into the deep spine, and becomes a steady upward flow toward the top of the head. This is a subtle aspect of these realities, however, and is less capable of being related to common experience. It would therefore be unsuitable to develop it further in the pages of this book, which is being written for the general public. Suffice it here to say that self-offering to God is more than a "good mood," and that withdrawal into the Self does not, in the deeper sense, make one sad! Instead of sadness, withdrawal becomes calm, inward recognition of high spiritual realities.

The Gregorian chant expresses, as does much devotional music in all religions, a melancholy yearning for higher-than-earthly fulfillment. This, again, is not sadness in the ordinary sense of the word, and its ultimate fulfillment is blissful union with God.

Knowledge of these subtle truths is extremely helpful for anyone seeking deeper understanding of spiritual law. That knowledge results in a science greater than any material science—one, indeed, deserving consideration as a science of all sciences, for the benefits it confers far outweigh anything promised in the earthly sciences. The science of religion, then, embraces much more than spiritual attitudes, important as these are. When the energy is directed upward to the brain, outward, worldly tendencies disappear as a matter of course.

Positive attitudes can be affirmed, and therefore reinforced, by sitting upright, holding the chest up, looking up, and breathing deeply. Right posture is not spiritually essential, in itself, but it naturally accompanies inspiration, and is, for most people, easily performed. Why not, then, cooperate with Nature? To ignore these facts with the pious rationale that one would rather depend on God's grace alone is, indeed, an indication of willful blindness. God, after all, gave us these laws. They should be taken as a sign of His grace, which can be used to facilitate spiritual progress. If anyone chooses instead to decide for himself how grace shall operate in his life, he must be considered either lazy, incompetent, or presumptuous! The saying, "God helps those who help themselves," applies very well in this case. Why not help oneself in any way possible, especially if the opportunity to do so has, so to speak, been served one on a silver platter? Wouldn't it be absurd to wait for God to chew and swallow the food one eats? Already He digests it through the energies provided by Nature in the body.

A bent spine is the enemy of spirituality. Another impediment is the tendency to gaze habitually downward. It is *possible,* of course, to pray with a bent back, as some people do who associate that position with humility. Stooping, however, obstructs the flow of energy in the spine. As for a downward gaze, some people may consider it proper in the presence of the Divine Majesty, and anything else a presumption. In fact, however, a downward gaze while praying and meditating takes the mind downward, not upward to God. Downwardness suggests a feeling of unworthiness, when in fact God *invites* the soul to soar. Stooping suggests a servile attitude also. Attitudes of unworthiness and servility are negative. They are not at all the same thing as humility. Humility, indeed, begins with *self-forgetfulness*. True humility uplifts the energy; it doesn't abase it. Any posture that obstructs that upward flow hinders the development of all ennobling attitudes, including humility.

There is another practice that initially appears purely physical, but that conduces greatly to spiritual development. It is to gaze, as well as concentrate, upward at the point between the eyebrows, the "spiritual eye." The eyes, in superconsciousness, turn naturally upward. Saints, therefore, are often depicted praying with their eyes upturned. They have frequently been observed in this position.

These are all simple practices, but invaluable for attaining ultimate bliss. Spiritual attitudes, as well, develop naturally with these practices. Best is a combination of the two: right spiritual attitude coupled with right technique.

Together, these two ensure steady and rapid progress on the spiritual path.

Ultimately, it must be added, what liberates the soul is divine grace. It is unrealistic, however, to claim that man plays no part in the process. Nectar cannot fill a chalice that is turned upside-down. One must *cooperate consciously with* grace. To wait passively for grace to descend may mean waiting a long, long time! Neither spinelessness, which is craven, nor arrant presumption can lead anyone to God.

The laws that govern the physical body are not affected by religious beliefs, as such, nor by the lack of them. The body works as it will, regardless. Moral principles, too, are determined by laws of human nature. How one responds to those principles determines one's own measure of happiness or unhappiness. Spiritual principles are not, however, *outside of* natural law. The saying, "Pride goes before a fall," is true for every kind of self-deception, and not for pride alone. No law of our own being can be circumvented. If a person wants to be happy, he must live according to the law. He cannot for instance eat nails with the rationalization that he possesses free will. And if he wants to be in tune with God's will, he must accept that certain aspects of that will have been presented to him already.

The true purpose of religion is to teach the law as it applies to one's spiritual life. No matter what religious tenets one holds, if he would know God he must direct his feelings upward from the heart to the spiritual eye, and focus them there in the expectation of bliss.

It would greatly increase people's general awareness of the brotherhood of the human race if religionists everywhere would focus on the universal aspects of truth, and were to concern themselves less with its variety of expressions. The great teachers of mankind have always shown an understanding of the law as it relates to human nature. They have taught the need for harmonizing one's life with that law. When they have sought to correct, it has never been to criticize one another's teachings, but to help rectify people's misunderstanding of various aspects of the truth. Man, alas, ever demonstrates a special talent for rationalizing his ignorance.

True teachers never, on the other hand, tell people, "Follow whatever concoction of spiritual teachings you yourself find appealing, for they are all the same." A city can be approached by many routes, but not by more than one route at a time. Faced with the decision as to which road to follow, usually one should follow whichever one leads inward from where he himself happens to be. We are speaking, of course, allegorically. Spiritually speaking, that place must be determined by one's own nature, and not by any geographical location. It will be helpful also to travel on a paved road, and not to strike out at random over an endless succession of cow pastures.

There is a safe way to estimate the validity of a teaching: It is to see whether the teaching corresponds to the wisdom of the past. For wisdom never conflicts with itself. It does happen, however, that some of the disciples of a great teacher seize upon certain aspects of his teachings, which to them seem unique, and on those grounds claim that his teachings are the best. Differences do exist, of course. Indeed, it is both natural and inevitable that they do. A teacher must, after all, address not only humanity as a whole, but a particular group of people at their particular time in history, and in their particular culture. His aim, always, is to bring them back to their individual "zero point." When they've strayed too far to the left, he tells them, "Go right." When they've strayed too far right, he teaches, "Go left." As a person rowing a small boat on the ocean must ride with the waves even while he pushes on toward his destination, so a master "rides with" people's lesser errors with a view to taking them in the long-range direction they need to pursue at the present time. Many disciples, unfortunately, let trivialities swallow up divine principles, as ocean waves obscure its deeps. Primarily, their aim is to support their own ego-inspired insistence on superiority.

Could God really want His human children to be narrow-minded? How could He, who created the vast universe, ignore that cosmic spectacle in favor of this one little mud ball, Earth? And, given this peculiar fascination, how would He scorn millennia of history and numberless civilizations before ours to bestow exclusive blessings on a handful of squabbling zealots, who cannot agree even among themselves how best to worship Him? Such "faith" would be ludicrous—were it not in need of compassion.

Children learn from their parents to avoid some of the perils they may encounter. In Indian villages, they learn to go carefully where cobras might lurk. Children all over the world learn the rules for keeping their bodies healthy, and how to behave toward others. The great teachers of mankind, similarly, speak of the pitfalls and rewards in morality. Their precepts on such matters all agree with one another.

Great teachers do not emphasize "disclosures" that are foreign to all common sense. Nor do they try to attract a following by making stunning "revelations" with a view to bewildering people with the exotic. They seek to reassure everyone that truth is man's native reality. Religion, rightly understood, is not a system of intricate rituals. Its purpose is simply to inspire love for that most relishable fulfillment possible: Conscious Bliss.

True teachings* are given to mankind as guides on the rocky pathway of life. Priests in every religion often insist that they are the sole heirs to divine revelation. Revelation, however, is born of insight, simply, derived from actual experience. In the Absolute, no question arises of good, better, or best; relativity is transcended. A master is above the three gunas, having attained oneness with the Absolute Spirit. How can he, in that state, be higher or lower than any other master? Indeed, interreligious rivalry blasphemes against divine love itself. God's love, far from being particular, holds the very stars on their course.

Ego-attachment brings an easy bias toward anything that one thinks might boost his self-importance. He likes to think of his path to

---

*I emphasize the word "true" here because not all religious teachings are equally valid. It is not enough merely to teach in the name of religion, or of God. There are religious teachers who, though famous and charismatic, have not themselves attained spiritual wisdom.

truth as the only right—or at any rate as the best—one. The first sign of a true teaching is its power to inspire. No inspiration arises from sectarian bickering. A teaching that has no inspiration cannot be of God. Rather, that very lack is evidence that it derives from ego-consciousness.

True teachings vibrate with spiritual power. They are not products of intellectual pondering, which at best offers only reasonable deductions. The profoundest philosophy can do no more than recommend: It cannot uplift.

A true spiritual teaching offers something else also: transcendence. It is a descent to earth of divine grace. Attunement with that ray of grace is transforming. It draws the aspirant up in light to the realm of superconsciousness. To ascend by any such ray, however difficult at first, becomes at last effortlessly liberating. True religion, then, is a manifestation God Himself sends for the redemption of mankind. To ignore the need for divine assistance is to reject the obvious, raising the question: Is it God one is serving, or is it one's own ego? For God doesn't act except through instruments. The very creation of worlds is accomplished through channels of light and energy. Nothing individual is created directly. Implanted in every living creature is the power to reproduce itself.

One thinks here of the farmer's reply when a priest said to him, "What a beautiful farm you and God have made here."

"I'm sure you're right, Father," the farmer answered. "But you should have just seen it when God had it all to Himself!"

God offers mankind upliftment through many channels: expansive scenery, inspiring books, beautiful music, wise teachers, corrective experiences. Were one to try to grow spiritually without any help of this sort, he might as well try to fly without wings!

A car engine must be given a spark by a starter for it to "turn over." The "engine" of human consciousness, similarly, needs sparking, to begin to function superconsciously. The "spark" must be delivered by someone with the power, himself, to administer it superconsciously. No mere philosopher, certainly, and no mere organization can transmit such power. This statement can be tested: Simply look into the eyes of people who have received actual spiritual blessing in their lives; then look into those of people who have remained satisfied with receiving good teachings without that additional ingredient of power. Life cannot be initiated by anyone who is sterile or impotent.

The highest mountain peak can never touch the overarching heavens. Human aspiration, similarly, no matter how sincere, can never touch the ethereal skies of spiritual perfection. The aspirant must rise on a ray sent down by God. One ray is sufficient, and a blessing not easily won. Without it, the ego would never be able to span the gulf separating it from infinity.

To try to soar on a multiplicity of rays would also be a mistake; it would indicate a lack of commitment. That commitment, moreover, must be mutual between the seeker and the "ray" itself. For the instrument of divine grace is conscious of his role, and serves in that capacity with extraordinary self-sacrifice. Eclecticism on the part of the divine aspirant indicates a lack both of serious purpose and of sensitive appreciation for the great concern for him on the part of the true teacher, whom God has asked to bring him to enlightenment.

God is not a Moslem, Christian, Jew, Buddhist, or Hindu. No enlightened soul is sectarian. If a Moslem, for example, deeply loves Allah, the great teachers of every religion will be equally pleased with him—Jesus Christ and Moses no less so than Mohammed. Indeed, Jesus Christ will be as pleased with him as with any Christian.

Spiritual religion differs in one respect above all from the ordinary methods for alleviating human sorrow: It recognizes man's utter need to depend on a Higher Power. Merely to believe in God's existence is, after all, no great compliment to Him! To accept actual divine guidance and inspiration, rather, through God's awakened channels, is what differentiates the sincere seeker from the dilettante.

True religion is a science. It shows how to find permanent freedom from all sorrow in the attainment of Conscious Bliss. True, spiritual religion offers the only workable solution there is to humanity's deepest needs, and for this reason deserves to be considered the science of all sciences. It is, indeed, the driving force behind all civilization, without which there would be no arts or sciences, but only a clumsy, cudgeling process of self-aggrandizement. Ego-boosting desires, unless directed upward toward bliss, are useless for the attainment of lasting happiness. People devote enormous amounts of energy to fulfilling such desires, often risking their very lives, but ignore the one thing they really care anything about: their own lasting happiness. Driven like paper boats on a pond by the hurricane of ambition, they founder repeatedly, suffering. Their every fulfillment is evanescent, as their little boat, so crisp and jaunty when first placed in the water, grows soggy and shapeless. In the garden of happiness, the flowers wither and turn lifeless by nightfall.

The science of religion is the *reasonable* aspect of spiritual teaching. Though reasonable and a science, it continues to emphasize the ennobling virtues, adding to them only the satisfaction of solid, practical proof.

Many thousands of years ago, in India, this science was developed under the name, *Yoga.* Yoga means "union," which is to say the complete integration of body, mind, and soul, resulting in union with Conscious Bliss. The essence of yoga is Kriya Yoga, the great technique I mentioned earlier. This, truly, is *Sanaatan Dharma,* the Way to Eternal Enlightenment.

People today think of scientists almost in caricature, imagining them white-coated, frowning, and grimly steeped in theories of mighty pith and moment, but never aware of anything to smile about in life. Surely it is time for this image to be refined. A narrowly intellectual approach to life ignores the heart's feelings. Such an approach has ever possessed but a fading life: It is now ready for burial! True understanding requires a combination of intellectual reasoning with intuitive (though not emotional) feeling. For wisdom is not merely logical: It is understanding born of direct experience of the Supreme Reality, which is infinite, eternal, Conscious Bliss.

CHAPTER ELEVEN

The Nature of Bliss

The ego cannot easily conceptualize the vast consciousness that brought it into existence. Christian theologians describe God as "wholly other": that is to say, completely different from His creation. Indeed, so He must be if one compares man's littleness with God's infinity; the theologians, certainly, are not "wholly" wrong! The *Bhagavad Gita,* India's greatest scripture, however, describes God as being "in everything, but not touched by anything." In this sense, and if everything came out of Him, how can those theologians be "wholly" right?

Light bulbs are powered by the same electric source, but they shine differently according to their wattage and coloring. Such is the ego. Every human being is conscious of being special, in the sense of separate from everything and everyone else — and the central actor in everything in which he is directly concerned. He sees God as not only separate from him, but as another reality altogether — in fact "wholly other," as the theologians say. Those learned men voice, with that expression, a perfectly normal human perception — one that is rooted at the same time, however, in ego-consciousness, not in wisdom.

The difference between man's ego and God is not one of kind, but only of direction. When his consciousness flows outward to the senses, he sees himself as distinctly separate and individual. When his attention is reversed, however, he discovers an inner *and essential* Self. This Self has no separative features to distinguish it, for it embraces the essence of existence itself, revealing that its once-separate identity was a delusion. At the same time, it achieves if anything an *increase* of self-identity: not separative and relative, but unitive. Self-awareness in both the limited, egoic and the universal sense is our eternal reality. The ego only confines our sense of that "I." In truth, one's real "I" is everywhere! When energy and consciousness are directed inward to the indwelling soul, body-consciousness is lost. Awareness expands to infinity. In that self-expanded state, one in no way loses his self-awareness. Rather, he becomes aware that he, himself, is infinite.

To know who we really are — in eternity, and not only for a few anguishing earth years —

we must withdraw our consciousness from sensory identity, which has defined our ego-consciousness. Even while living in ego-consciousness, we must think of ourselves as the heirs of Infinity. The better we succeed in identifying ourselves with the soul rather than with this little body and personality, the more real for us will become the words of the master Jesus Christ, who declared, "I and my Father are one."

Human beings prefer to think in static, rather than in directional, terms. They believe they need the fixed definitions of reason, rather than the flowing awareness of intuition. Whatever man sees, therefore, he endows with individuality. He sees a wooden chair, and thinks it is quite different from the tree from which it came. Clouds seem to him altogether different from fast-flowing rivers, though he knows that both are made of the same substance. Modern science has told us not only that trees and chairs may be made of the same substance—a fact that has always been known—but that wood is essentially no different from the water in clouds and rivers, or from shining gold. A loaf of bread might, theoretically at least, be reabsorbed into the energy of which it is simply a vibration, and be re-manifested as a bar of gold. Science has not yet made the leap in this case from theory to demonstrated fact, but one sees no reason to doubt that the leap will be made, someday.

It is also a leap for man to change his perception of himself as a separate ego, conscious only in his brain, to the expanded perception that consciousness itself is infinite. If consciousness, however, is only *manifested through* the brain, rather than created by the brain—even as energy is *manifested through* matter but is not the creation *of matter*—then consciousness cannot be the mere product of the brain—perhaps by some as-yet-undefined process of secretion!

To be able to define truth is not necessarily the same thing as to be wise. Definitions are only abstractions of what they define. Defined truths are dogmas. Actual, direct perception of the truth is wisdom. Thus too, merely to describe the taste of an orange is very different from actually tasting it. (Try slaking your thirst on that description!) An egotist, persuaded intellectually that everything manifests consciousness but holding that concept only theoretically, might decide that he himself created everything that exists! Philosophical "greenhorns" there are who actually make such a claim: They say the whole universe, when they die, will cease to exist, since they themselves projected it, in thought.

This notion is easy to demolish. Such unripe theorists might ask themselves, simply, "Could I, myself, have personally designed and built the pyramids? the Taj Mahal? the Eiffel Tower? the Golden Gate Bridge? Could I, in my little person, have written the plays of Shakespeare? composed the symphonies of Beethoven? painted Leonardo's 'Last Supper?'" If anyone answers such questions by saying, "Why not?" ask him to create *just one* living leaf. Modern scientists boast that if they can only create so sophisticated an artificial intelligence that it will equal in every respect the brain-power of man, they will have produced consciousness itself. Let them contemplate a less exacting challenge: the humble worm. Could any artificial intelligence—which surely is not so far, even now, from replicating the intelligence of a worm— produce even so basic a degree of self-awareness as one sees in earthworms? They might succeed in simulating the *reactions* of worms, which are more or less automatic, but there is even in worms a measure of self-direction which shows them to be more than mechanisms. Consciousness produces the material channels needed for its expression. Matter cannot produce consciousness any more than matter is the *source* of energy. Nor can a limited consciousness produce the works of a greater consciousness.

Obviously, if the universe is indeed, as Sir James Jeans proposed, "mind stuff," that "stuff" was not produced by any mechanism. Nor was it produced by the all-but-microscopic ego! We are figments of God's conscious dream. It is not we ourselves who have produced that dream. Our awareness of an individual existence in this dream is not self-produced: It is derived from Him. The wave cannot rightly say, "I am the ocean." All it can claim is, "The ocean is my essential Self, which has manifested all the little waves of appearances, including my own little wave of self-consciousness, which I define as my ego."

Modern psychology, heavily influenced by Charles Darwin's Theory of Evolution, points downward: to the subconscious and to our animal origins, claiming that there lies our basic reality. The spiritual teachings, on the other hand, point upward. They insist that the superconscious is our true source, and that the *divine* is our true reality. These very opposite opinions, based on opposing directions of consciousness, are no mere figures of speech. Consciousness, as it becomes increasingly refined, actually rises in the spine, becoming centered at last in the frontal lobe of the brain and at the top of the head. The more animalistic a person's consciousness, the more fully his energy is centered in the lower part of his spine. "Earthy" people, often praised for their supposed realism, display by their very posture, their gestures, that their awareness is centered in their lower being as though radiating outward from their hips. Even when they converse, they make constant references to the lower functions of the body.

One feels pleasure when the energy is stimulated in the nerves, as one feels pain when the stimulation is excessive. Animals feel pleasure in the lower portion of their bodies, where nerves radiate outward from the lower centers in the spine. They have yet to awaken energy in the upper centers. Dogs, for instance, show their delight by wagging their tails; sometimes they even agitate vigorously their entire lower bodies. Human beings, also, if their pleasures are centered primarily in their lower spines, may wiggle their hips when they feel delighted for any reason! Stimulation of energy in the lower spine arouses the desire for such physical pleasures as sex and food. The more people's energy is stimulated in the lower spine, the more their lower nature is activated.

Stimulation of the lower centers of awareness, however, although to some extent pleas-

urable, conflicts with the desire all human beings have for happiness. This conflict increases
their awareness of the dualistic opposites:
pleasure and pain, happiness and suffering. By
giving more energy to the downward movement, one subjects himself to the opposite emotional states. Intense pleasure alternates,
inevitably, with intense pain.

When the energy is free to rise unobstructed
toward the brain, without any downward-
pulling material desires and impulses to hinder
it, one's consciousness soars heavenward in
bliss. Release comes from egoic limitations, for
one's consciousness expands one's self-identity.
This upward flow is crucially important to spiritual development. When awareness and energy are centered at the point between the
eyebrows, and rise thence to the highest center
at the top of the head, the consciousness of duality disappears, and the soul merges into the
oneness of Spirit.

The unending swing of the pendulum, left
and right with every rising and descending cur-
rent in the superficial spine, is nullified by rest
in the deep spine. The consciousness of duality
must be resolved, next, by raising the energy
from matter-attachment in its center at the base
of the spine to the state of spiritual union at the
top of the head: the *sahasrara,* as this highest

center is called in the yoga teachings.*

There are specific methods, as I mentioned in the last chapter, for accomplishing this upliftment. Connecting the inhalation and exhalation with the upward and downward movements of energy in the superficial spine, which is the origin of the sympathetic nervous system, those two movements are neutralized in breathlessness. The energy then no longer reacts to outer stimuli, and feelings of acceptance and rejection cease to trouble the mind. One experiences a unidirectional movement of rising energy in the deep spine, lifting him toward superconsciousness.

These subtle insights cannot be gained from books, but only from people who have attained high levels of consciousness, themselves. Great mystics in every religion have demonstrated their knowledge of these truths. The science of yoga, too, is as universal as algebra (which, incidentally, originated also in India). Jesus Christ certainly was familiar with *yogic* principles, and repeatedly demonstrated his familiarity with them. We see it, for example, in his statement,

---

*Interestingly, Saint Teresa of Avila in *The Interior Castle* (the first chapter of "The Fourth Mansion") described the top of the head as the seat of the soul. She wrote here also, "The spirit seems to move upward [toward this point] with great velocity." —JDW

"Lift up your eyes, and look on the fields; for they are white already to harvest." (John 4:35) This advice referred to the method of concentration alluded to in the last chapter, of focusing one's energy and concentration in the spiritual eye, between the eyebrows.*

A commitment of feeling to this upward flow is essential. That is why I've emphasized bliss in this book. Bliss is not only the best definition of God: It also offers mankind the strongest possible motive for seeking Him. God is, in very fact, for everyone, for what everyone seeks, consciously or unconsciously, is simply bliss.

God cannot be known, however, by mere definitions! He can be known only when energy and consciousness are united one-pointedly in concentration on Him.

The reader may have wondered occasionally why, considering my special focus on God as bliss, there are so many spiritual writings that

---

*I have presented a comprehensive study of the basics of yoga in a book, *The Art and Science of Raja Yoga,* based on the teachings of Paramhansa Yogananda. It is available from Crystal Clarity Publishers, Nevada City, California 95959. Others of what might be called the more *yogic* teachings of Jesus Christ are presented in another book of mine, also based on the teachings of Paramhansa Yogananda: *The Promise of Immortality in the Bible and the Bhagavad Gita,* available from the same publisher. — *JDW* describe Him as Love. God has eight essential aspects, in fact. Of these, Love and Bliss are only two. The other six are Wisdom, Peace, deep Calmness,* Power, Light, and Sound. Cosmic Sound is referred to in many scriptures. In Hinduism it is called AUM. The Bible speaks of it as the Amen, and also as the Word (in the first verse of St. John's Gospel[†]), and as "a noise of many waters."[‡]

Many saints have experienced God as Love. People of less highly developed consciousness, however, may encounter a certain problem in seeking Him above all for love, for their experience of love is as an emotion. Generally, in fact, people confuse love with ego-attachment. In Spanish, for example, the expression, "I love you," is, "*Te quiero* (I desire you)." The Indian scriptures do in fact sanction a romantic relationship with God, but this relationship must be developed with great purity of heart, with no hint of egoism, and certainly without a breath

---

*Calmness differs from peace in that calmness radiates deep power. Peace is, in one sense, more negative, for the deeply soothing satisfaction that comes with it lies in the release of one's consciousness from all sensory excitation.

[†]"In the beginning was the Word, and the Word was with God, and the Word *was* God."

[‡]Ezekiel 43:2.

of sexual desire. To try to develop a relationship with God as a devotional romance can, otherwise, be spiritually dangerous, for it may take the mind downward, awakening desires for ego-gratification.* The true goal of spiritual development is *transcendence,* particularly of the ego. For this reason it is better to love God as Bliss above all, for the very nature of bliss is impersonal. Love's true fulfillment in any case is bliss. It is safer and wiser, therefore, to make love a secondary goal in the quest for God.

The center of feeling is, as I have said, the heart. Love must be directed upward from that point to the spiritual eye, where the inner light awaits every seeker. Without this upward direction, the heart's feelings, once awakened, may become dissipated in outwardness. Intensely devotional feelings can dissipate themselves also in tears, unless devotion is kept under control and its energy directed upward rather than outward. Until one has mastered these princi-

---

*The best-known example of romantic love in the Indian scriptures appears in the stories of Krishna and the *gopis* (girl cowherds). The stories are allegorical. In fact, Krishna as described in them was only a child at the time, and the *gopis* were young married women, loyal to their husbands. The stories themselves, then, were not intended literally as tales of romance, but were allegories of the soul's loving relationship with God, meant to inspire humanity to understand that even romantic love can be fulfilled perfectly in God alone.

ples, he may, to his surprise, find himself plunged into spiritual error as the heart's energy is drawn downward suddenly by some "karmic bomb": an unexpected tendency that manifests itself in the mind. His heart's energy must, therefore, be directed deliberately — even, to some extent, austerely — upward to God.

Bliss, it must be understood finally, is very different from delight, such as the relief that comes after prolonged suffering. People may describe this relief as "blissful," but in fact it is only an emotional release, and therefore superficial. Never should one mistake bliss for the emotions, which fluctuate constantly. When bliss appears, one instantly recognizes it as the most central of all truths. Even nirvana, which connotes the complete cessation of all suffering, is only a prelude to the conscious bliss of *Satchidananda*. The end of suffering means not a cessation of consciousness itself, as many Buddhists believe.* Rather, it spells *finis* to duality itself, bringing the perfection of fulfillment in absolute bliss. There cannot ever be a cessation of consciousness itself, for there is nothing

---

*Would anyone strive earnestly to attain *nothingness?* One hardly believes so. The closer one approached it, surely, the greater would be his inclination to defer the total termination of everything!

in existence *except* consciousness!

The Buddha's compassion, then, which all Buddhists praise, as do all who know anything of his inspiring life, was — *and still is* — consequent upon his perfect awareness, not upon his complete — indeed, completely impossible! — unawareness. Buddha was certainly no atheist! It is his followers only who contribute this misunderstanding to the complex display of errors in the showcase of religious history. Buddha's followers misunderstood his unwillingness to speak of God. He was only trying to emphasize his central message, that man, too, must make a spiritual effort, and must not leave all his purification to divine grace. Moreover, he emphasized also that the Vedic fire rituals are only symbols of human upliftment. They are known as *karmakand,* and are not, themselves, directed toward the highest enlightenment, but only toward self-purification and the fulfillment of primarily human desires.

Bliss fulfills the deeper need for complete freedom from all suffering, *and for freedom in absolute completion.* Everyone wants eternal, and not merely transitory, bliss. God alone as Conscious Bliss can satisfy that perpetual craving. Everyone wants bliss of a kind that will never grow tiresome, in time, as all other fulfillments do. (Consider how even the most beautiful music becomes irritating, if one hears it for too long.) The best possible definition of God, then, is *Ever-Existing, Ever-Conscious, Ever-New Bliss.* Bliss is what all are already seeking, though few are aware that it is their actual goal. By loving God as bliss one can develop the intense devotion that seems, to many, so heroic an aspect of the lives of saints.

Bliss cannot even be *attained,* really. The soul simply realizes that bliss is, eternally, its own nature. For bliss simply *is.* It is what remains after everything else disappears. Bliss is the eternal, forever unchanging reality which underlies the whole universe. All things, including all other aspects of God, are contained in Conscious Bliss. They merge into, and become, eternal, Conscious Bliss.

What the aspirant must do is make happiness, first, then joy, and finally bliss his constant reality. How can you do that? I would like to offer this suggestion:

Every time a bubble of happiness appears in your heart, make it your priority. Cling to your awareness of it! The cause of that happiness may be entirely commonplace — even the fulfillment of some perfectly trivial desire. Whatever its source, enjoy the happiness as a thing in itself. Forget whatever caused it, outwardly. Mentally expand that bubble every time you exhale. Watch the bubble grow larger. Dwell on the joy contained in it. Separate that joy from any limiting definition of it. For remember, true joy can never be confined. It has no boundaries. Its center is everywhere; its circumference, nowhere. *Become* joy itself. Be no longer contained within even the rainbow bubble of your happiness! *You are Absolute Bliss itself!*

By dwelling ever more deeply on the awareness of the essential joy of your own being, you will find the barriers of confining consciousness breaking down, and bliss itself streaming outward in all directions. Let bliss release you in infinity.

The goal of this book has been to inspire you to seek God as Conscious Bliss. The attainment of bliss will be your final proof of everything I have proclaimed:

God is, indeed, for everyone!

PARAMHANSA YOGANANDA

Paramhansa Yogananda was born in 1893 in India. His line of gurus sent him to America in 1920, where, during the 1920s, he became quite possibly the best-known public speaker. In 1946 he published his world-famous *Autobiography of a Yogi,* which has sold millions of copies and, in eighteen translations, is still (in 2003) one of the best-known and best-selling spiritual books in the world. In addition he wrote several other books, all of them classics in the field of religion and spirituality.

In 1925 Paramhansa Yogananda founded Self-Realization Fellowship, a worldwide organization headquartered on Mt. Washington in Los Angeles, California.

Yogananda during his lifetime attracted many thousands of students and disciples. He is generally considered today one of the leading spiritual figures of our times.

J. DONALD WALTERS (SWAMI KRIYANANDA)

J. Donald Walters (Swami Kriyananda) has been a disciple of Paramhansa Yogananda's since 1948. He has given thousands of lectures over the years in many countries, acquainting people with his Guru's teachings. In addition, he has written over eighty books and edited two books of Yogananda's which have become well known: *The Rubaiyat of Omar Khayyam Explained* and a compilation of sayings of the Master, *The Essence of Self-Realization.* Among his other books is his autobiography, *The Path,* which describes his three and a half years of discipleship under the great Guru until Yogananda's death in 1952. All of these activities have been in obedience to his guru's personal instructions.

In 1968 Walters founded an intentional community near Nevada City, California, based on the teachings of Paramhansa Yogananda. The community's name is Ananda. Since then, Walters has founded five other Ananda communities in four American states, and one in Italy, where he lives at present.

INDEX

Absolute Spirit
  as basis of creation, 142, 145–48
  center of, 146
  individualized, soul as, 143

Abstract perceptions, 18, 21

Advaita (non-dualism)
  defined, 34–35
  devotion and, 35–36, 37
  dreams and, 35
  Vaishnavas and, 39–40

Ahankara, 179. *See also* Ego

Allah, 30, 43

Amen, 119, 210

Anahat chakra. *See* Heart center

Ananda. *See* Bliss (*Ananda*)

Angels, 41

Attachment
  to body, 163–65
  causing suffering, 163–65, 169–70
  habits and, 169–70
  mental detachment vs., 169
  to pleasures/happiness, 83–88,
    169–70
  survival and, 164–65

Attention, centering, 93

Augustine, Saint, 40, 84

AUM
  hearing, 39, 119, 210
  as name of God, 39, 210

Authority
  questioning, 129–33
  in religion, 122–25, 129–33

Awareness. *See* Self-awareness

Behavior, principles of, 45

Beliefs
  faith vs., 32
  as hypotheses, 32
  testing religious, 26–27, 32

Bhagavad Gita, 73, 200

Bliss (*Ananda*), 34
  absoluteness of, 83–84, 97
  of Buddha, 93–94, 97

challenges of, 82–83
defined, 212
driving evolution, 49–50
eternal nature of, 81
evolving awareness of, 50
experiencing, technique, 214–15
false notion of, 85–88, 139
flow of, 69, 214–15
God as, 209
as highest goal, 211, 215
as innate, 49
love becoming, 132–33
in lower life forms, 50, 55–56
material desires and, 63
as motivator, 209
nature of, 211–15
non-attachment and, 63–64, 169,
  170
referencing, 64
resistance to, 83–88
steadfastness of, 133–34
survival vs., 49–50
unboundedness of, 214–15
upward energy for, 181, 182–83,
  185, 186–88, 189, 207–9, 211
will power for, 92, 93–94, 97
as zero point, 169
See also Conscious Bliss; Happiness

Bose, Jagadis Chandra, 140–41

Breath, 184, 185–86, 208

Buddha
  compassion of, 213
  Conscious Bliss and, 111
  on death, 96
  encouraging self-effort, 33–34, 41,
    97
  enlightenment of, 48
  Great Vow of, 93–94, 99
  misconceptions about teaching of,
    33–34
  as personal Savior, 23, 45
  worship and, 106

Buddhi, 179. *See also* Intellect

Buddhism
  devotion and, 35

RECOMMENDED BOOKS, MUSIC,
AND OTHER RECORDINGS

BOOKS BY AND ABOUT
PARAMHANSA YOGANANDA

AUTOBIOGRAPHY OF A YOGI
*The best-selling autobiography of Yogananda that has
inspired millions of people worldwide (also available
as an audio book, read by Swami Kriyananda)*

THE ESSENCE OF SELF-REALIZATION
A collection of wise sayings by Yogananda

THE RUBAIYAT OF OMAR KHAYYAM EXPLAINED
*A commentary on this famous text by Paramhansa
Yogananda (also available as an audio book, read by
Swami Kriyananda)*

RECORDINGS

THE BIRD OF TIME
Selections from Yogananda's book THE RUBAIYAT
OF OMAR KHAYYAM EXPLAINED *read by J. Donald Walters, with accompaniment from the music
album,* I, Omar, *also by J. Donald Walters*

BOOKS BY J. DONALD WALTERS
(SWAMI KRIYANANDA)

THE PATH
One Man's Quest on the Only Path There Is
An autobiography, with hundreds of stories of life with Paramhansa Yogananda

THE PROMISE OF IMMORTALITY
The True Teaching of the Bible and the
Bhagavad Gita

AWAKEN TO SUPERCONSCIOUSNESS
Meditation for Inner Peace, Intuitive Guidance,
and Greater Awareness

OUT OF THE LABYRINTH
For Those Who Want to Believe, but Can't

HOPE FOR A BETTER WORLD!
The Small Communities Solution

THE HINDU WAY OF AWAKENING
Its Revelation, Its Symbols

ART AS A HIDDEN MESSAGE
A Guide to Self-Realization

A PLACE CALLED ANANDA
The trial by fire that forged one of the most successful cooperative communities in the world today

THE ART AND SCIENCE OF RAJA YOGA
Fourteen steps to higher awareness based on the teachings of Yogananda

MUSIC CDS BY DONALD WALTERS:

CHRIST LIVES – *an Oratorio*

WINDOWS ON THE WORLD
Songs inspired by many countries, sung by the composer

I, OMAR
Inspired by Paramhansa Yogananda's book, THE RUBAIYAT OF OMAR KHAYYAM EXPLAINED

KRIYANANDA CHANTS YOGANANDA
Many chants by Yogananda and Kriyananda, sung by Swami Kriyananda

EACH ONE—REACH ONE!

There are special books that can change lives—this is one of them! Perhaps you have a friend, family member, or co-worker to whom you'd like to give this book. Join our Each One—Reach One campaign, and uplift the world one person at a time.

To help in this effort we're extending a **special offer**. We will provide you with additional copies of this book (as many as you like) at **50% off** the cover price. Order your **half price** copies today directly from Crystal Clarity Publishers.

❦

To Place an order, request a free Crystal Clarity catalog, or to receive our complimentary e-newsletter, you can reach us at:

Crystal Clarity Publishers
800-424-1055 (or) 530-478-7606
Or visit our website, complete with secure, online ordering at: www.crystalclarity.com

❦

If you find this book inspiring and would like to learn more about the life and teachings of Paramhansa Yogananda, there are many resources available. Please contact:

Ananda Sangha
14618 Tyler Foote Rd.
Nevada City, CA 95959
(530) 478-7560 ananda@ananda.org
www.ananda.org